ANTHONY HOWELL

COLLECTED LONGER POEMS

Anthony Howell

Collected Longer Poems

1969–2023

Grey Suit Editions

Published in 2024
by Grey Suit Editions, an affiliate
of Karnac Books Limited

British Library Cataloguing in Publication Data
A C.I.P. catalogue record for this book is available
from the British Library

Paperback ISBN: 978-1-903006-37-5
e-book ISBN: 978-1-903006-38-2

Designed and typeset by Anvil

Printed and bound in the United Kingdom
by Hobbs the Printers Ltd

Grey Suit Editions
33 Holcombe Road, London N17 9AS
https://greysuiteditions.co.uk/

Contents

Sergei de Diaghileff (1929)

'Seroja, you're hurting. Hurt me!' Ach – I worried his arm
Against the dull class; trapped, worming, a
Wrist beneath lid. Provincial towns – Perm,
The desk-lid: grained geology of an Ernst or Dubuffet,
Neither of whom I admire. And no metaphor
Making of it a made theme. Compass-bored, elaborate
With sly graffiti. Myself bored with compasses.
Litter classified, schooling: 'Those cusps, crimped
Leaves; crisp as yeasty outside the window
They curl skyward. Say it. Say it!' – I levered him –
'Mathematics is unrussian!' Chinchilla.
And that was the one and only time the brigadier
Thrashed me. (Seroja broke my arm sir, he said . . .
He said) One duel I championed nature: memento.
Now strut, cultivate the strand.

'Je suis le spectre . . .' Gautier now. But what gold
Paved Peter's town! I skated, plump and suave.
Composition does not become me, since Rimsky insists.
Why not compose my friends? Mutely, imported aquarelles
Ignite the Stieglitz. That was before I invented
The avant-garde. 'Mir Isskoustva' . . . or some such aesthetic
Lab. Test-tubes to bung up Fokine, Benois
(Poor souls). I drew on my pipette and played them:
Compounded one with another to produce
That nonsense 'Armide': (effoliate the pavilion,
Tree-trunks as Louis XIV chair legs). Consider me
Neither as amateur nor dilettante. Am

The catalyst. Vatza decidedly
Lost his pants. The Czarina ruffled (that was that).

The rose disrobes. I stripped the epiderm.
Never left nature her own devices (uncunning
Streams, leaves, have none). But folklorique as always
Our Russian brigades stormed the pelted,
Pelting tiers – where Astruc alternates blond with brunette.
The Châtelet repainted. No time to notice
Parisian May, I lounged in the stalls exhaustless.
'Je suis le spectre . . . 'If so, Théophile, I shall haunt
Those stalls. Always to peel, to redefine,
In the light of the latest prodigy, my malaise.
With less of an idea have now than had,
What constitutes. So many prodigies have modified
Since then. Where Cocteau rhymes to define
Nijinsky dances. Oh, the dread and horror of their task!
My own abilities hinder. All theirs is mine, my
Papillions, pastiches. Wand white I have abandoned.

Now wheel me out on the veranda. Those,
Incidentally charcoals, are by – but of course you know.
Breathing! How I care more now (late my day)
For air. But not too clear and rare and precious.
This hot-house of a lagoon suits me, with
Its air fin-de-siècle and unhealthy. ' . . . de la rose
Que tu portais hier . . . ' which I carried,
Have abandoned. Carry the spectre.
Reproach my self-indulgent tears, while what's
His wife's name? Romola? – stupid, stupid

As a woman, as the droves of swans, gulls, geese,
Heckled and departed in their own brief lights

To clack in frippery: fluttering companies
Which ignore the lighthouse! Pavlova. And that
White pear, that Rubenstein! With just as much mobility
As a pear, whereas to be danced
Around she made a fine shrine. Must have
Her way and rolls about the stage – to Stravinsky
(The one man Rimsky might allow compose,
And who repaid him kindly!). Poire en lieu de grenade
Was gingered. Sugary through and all through
That fool Leon! As Romola: 'Jew to be sure,
But he was also something of a genius.' (Bakst).
How should *she* know (of genius)? From the day
Her 'rose' proposed she was at sea. The ninny!

'...que tu portais hier... au bal.' Spectre,
This morning shall preamble. A blue God
Incenses me in the Lido... Make those French windows
Taller, take away the bird! The rose's elevation
Elevates. Should seem incongruous he remind me here,
A creature essentially Russian? Not so
Incongruous to be here perhaps? Hand me those delights
Which tease my doctors – follow my finger, over where
A boy rises on his toes – those insteps – as the foam
Covers them, at the Lido's margin; leotard
For swim-suit. A Picasso. (Do you know him? Has designed
Several.) See him for himself, unsigned. A body by Nijinsky.

'Vatza, mais tu es paresseux.' Purr, purr,
'Mais viens, viens. J'ai besoin de toi.' 'Je ne peux pas
Car je suis fou' Listen to Sergio recite his visions
'Du Baller Russe'. Vatza, Vatza
Has taught me how body is sterner,
More morally severe than mind bewitched
By lascivious environs: mimosa
Shaking its plaits over the hill's shoulder, something
In the air; immediate realisation of breathing this or that
Crisp morning; pillars emerge from mist – how body
May refuse, say look, say listen to the first,
The first ray, bird wing skip the water, the first motes
Rising serenely on their long journey to the sun. That day
In obese mirrored, guilty apartment. Moscow:
My art-junk; too many icons, long since abandoned,
Forgot. Me naked. Him naked
And his eyes. I would have pomaded, paraded before that mirror,
Instead, his body's remonstrance. I parodied.
For his oblique eyes drew lids, for once revealing
Stavemarks where a Slav tune trod adagio and lightly,
To which his fear was counterpoint;
A spoiling innovation, nervously nouveau. He had

A body on him which could utter – I'm losing words. Help
Me drink . . . better. Yes, could utter at its most inactive
(Seated, say shifting slightly the weight), or most riotous
'Igor', a complete silence as of the steppe
Pacing, pacing effortlessly towards invisible pole.
He spoke with such a lump in the mouth
There must have been God in him. And the God

Was body – but not a permissive, Bacchic –
A 'but', admitting of no excesses, sighing for all the world
His nailed limbs. A question, anxious for his starved
Beasts taken for glue in the factories
Whose smoke spirals, nooses the steppe in hemp.
(And the noose closed on the dancer.)

The mirror tarnished. Room shrank from his presently
Into frowsy antiques. Routed, the array of china,
Bell-tassels, gaslit candelabra… Diabetic now in Venice,
The white Russian with the lacquered hair
And a taste for… certain tastes is, am still, abashed.
The God, my Hellenic reason, stared me
Down. Failed my slipshod, already corpulent.
I, the eloquent, darling of every spa from Dieppe to 'Petrograd',
Say with my body, what? The neurotic flesh
Speechless than incoherent compared to his. A
Congenital vegetable! The intelligence,
Knowledge and memory in his flesh. It was Stravinsky.

Was the Urals, shawled, with no more fathers,
Husbands, sons, left to bury.
And the paradox: a Romany whore, swings bells,
Roubles, bosom, back to her surly. (Also the bull lines
Somewhere; the sad circus's attic animalry
Of that young Spaniard mentioned earlier. His
Primary blue, his Mediterranean 'as above Gourdon
That day.' His centaurs stamping
The beach). Was river, sky, pine-sweat,
But would not use these as a seasonal excuse

For poetry, the legs' laughter, clothes strewn
Over a rug… My cigar
Singed an overweight chair.

I dressed shabbily. Remember how his hand
Reached for, held, turned the door handle.
Then the door closed. The door
Has remained closed. It took some time to conquer
My body's shyness, his own temerity
In these matters. But the door refused, refuses
When tenement crumbles. Water!
He became confident, sly. We were several times,
How many hours, I can assure you, happy.
But I, my body, never learnt that language.
For with the first closing of a kiss something else
Should open. Darkness be broken into like a tomb.
I never hooked fingers, tugged and prised

My lazar house. Inarticulate half moan, the most
My preserved limbs managed – after intense effort –
Words as if for water, loudless, infirm, less
Free than my throat hobbles them now.
And that once i may imagine (only) remember
In Paris. Had no desire to dominate but to speak.
To speak, keep with me. (This afternoon
Rodin invites you as a faun to his conservatory).
To keep him, dominate, in some way: silence.

A death at sea? I venture to the shore,
No further; was a death certainly

Aboard ship – his departure.
How the meaningful sea has deceived me.
With Amérique du Sud, engagement, exile.
I puffed up silky: an extremely clumsy panther, dumb with body, rage;
Having become powerful in his world.
Now R introduces him to acupuncturists
While I weep – petulantly.

More Nijinskys, noces; more strident origins, more
Prodigious Russians. All prodigal: bitches, cocktail hours,
Balanchines. I know few dancers (and I have known many
In several ways) who could approach his mother tongue,
Which nothing trains nor breeds. Have seldom spoke
So guileless when I say, Have seen
Such speech. Any may dance, but rhetorically. Who knows
If style is what matters, especially now,
Since I turned bookish, shelving...?

Venice sets as the sun raises a haze.
Glimmer of hooves, St Mark's drawn into fog.
The day raises sandy and treacherous.   That boy,
Towelled after his morning, mounts the frail,
The soon to be footed shore. Here I am,
Spectator of my last cotillion; a
Portly butterfly, sedate above the spume. Frail wings
In the mist – a perfect Balanchine? – Merde!
Water me. Ramasse mes oreillers!

Femina Deserta

The Maker takes his one siesta
In this idle country bare
Of milk and honey, mud and straw:

A garden where the presence of
Proprietor diminishes
The space elsewhere embedding things.

Does meditation magnify
A moment or elaborate
Events to dress the poverty?

The mind's a spider in this heat:
Metaphor's geometry
Must extend a lengthy net,

Whose rigging may intend towards
A hillock where a certain bush
Is said to quench the thirst with fire –

But nomads in retirement stare
Beyond the littered littoral
Where shepherds reprimand their sheep:

They tell of cairns reviewing cairns
Already seen, and further still
A riddle waving eager tall:

Underneath whose haunches fur
Explains the smell that captivates
Aroma conscious Bedouin:

Holding a breath for ever and ever,
Saturating lungs
Jealous of what each inhales.

Pernicious breeze in nostrils able
To divine a lost oasis
By the reek of its mirage.

Here Solitude herself remains
Inert – for all the splash of pails
In the well available.

Guess ahead, suppose a city
Helmeted with mosque,
Flinging the lance of its minaret.

But will a hand succeed in crossing
Such a virginal expanse
While struggling against repose?

Perhaps the never pictured mosque
Which rinses clean all vision stained
By naked light cannot appear?

The further place forbids a visit:
Dwellers there may be supposed
To own no word for boundary;

Where afternoons direct migrations,
And each profile of tall bone
Gives away an obvious name,

And if and when a finger twitches
Surfaces of satin stir
In hieroglyphic labyrinths.

But as we near the stranger stars
Our singers cease to innovate,
They pause at more familiar nouns.

A savage blaze upon the forehead
Of a brigand's horse describes
That ambush which the sun prepares:

Before whose rampant haze the date road
Falters. Our approach explodes
The landmarks – into old dry birds.

The desert thinks the vultures limping
Over her reflection are
The pockmarks of her dry oases.

Horror in the gleam of joy
That blinds the fly who crawls among
Her lips towards a laser tongue!

At arm's length is the sun whose grin
Certifies he values her
Above his other predators.

She turns away, inviting night's
Brown eyelids down to soothe the shells
Azure as mosques, her nested eyes.

Hip to hip she lies with night
Though envious of the splendid gouts
Replenishing his open mouth

Her own reserve is curdled somewhere
Silent – and for this her nerves
Must go to vague extremities.

That she may blossom at the tight
Antipodes of every root
Sky becomes a tree of rain:

A thunder tree that clenches cloud,
The torso of a liquid god
Which branches out in muscled flood,

And shakes the fledglings from her shells
Till tunes revolve like little pins
Arranged around a cylinder.

The desert stretches forth her neck
And shifts her weight – a sluggish ocean
Pleased the rudder alters her.

Then cacti germinate and fix
Their set of brooches there before
The miracle evaporates

In sand whose tautly hollow sound
Is evidence, although an ear
Will never prove the reservoir.

Such secrecy envenoms flesh
And suckles what prefers to wriggle
Like a vein, immersed in dust.

No faithful dove invades these waves
To whisper the obscenities
Of any charming rainbow demon.

Flash! The thunder came and went.
That momentary deluge seemed
A phantom of annunciation.

Mockeries of vegetation
Are engendered thus, to jilt
Her thirstiness and leave her frozen.

Leave her freezing in the sun
Whose cymbals deafen when they clash,
While fever beats its rapid drum:

Fever which insists mosquitoes
Darn upon her famished realm
A needle-pointed zodiac:

Because without one stitch of green
Embroidery, spread-eagled, bound
By thongs which tighten while they dry.

A kind of shame, the drought chastises
Wilderness, that naked ground
Where revelations feel their way.

Attitudes at Altitudes

I

Doors open automatically as you encounter
Their all-seeing eye or step on a mat.
You glance up at a complicated flight
Notification board, abstractedly watching
Cities go flickering up the shutters.
For speed and safety, or to combat crime,
There are double layers of glass, double
Yellow lines, terrorist traps, prohibitive
Ordinances. Tickets are separated from
Counterfoils, travellers from families,
Husbands decide upon off-duty luxuries,
Musak is interrupted by gate allocation,
Overnight cases trail on detachable castors.
After the last cuddles and rubber stamps
You walk away from missed opportunities,
Bad moves, broken partnerships, onto flat,
Lettered tarmac where your Kraken sits
Buttressed by motorised steps. It sucks
On fuel straws, takes air into quadruplet
Wheels; its low slung, bosomy engines
Awaiting pressure on a button which ignites
Their only indrawn breath. It lifts open
Sections of curved carapace to pop in
Pills of baggage or let on passenger mites.
These mites have invented their host.

They watch the emergency ballet, fasten
Themselves in, crane sideways to peer out
Or sink back to stare at the diagrams
And the vomit bag in the pouch at the back
Of the seat ahead. Their flimsy caboodle
Turns on the spot and fumbles an arrow
Under the blue sky. Taxiing over a space
Fringed with palm trees or low buildings
It leaves behind its bumboat flotilla of
Service vehicles. There is a pause for grace, '
Then the surge forward, gathering courage
Past flashes of control tower, fuel depot,
Until momentum floats them on the wing,
And the creature ingests its own undercarriage.

    2

Thread fences, insect commercial districts,
Layouts for new estates, mudflats, a few
Trees dwindling to pinheads. Our shadow
Hurries over the refinery's neat tins,
A delicate fern of ripples behind a boat,
Stadium oval, slip-road arabesque, high-rise
Crystallising on the tight bend of a river
– Tiny cranes gesticulating from the top
Of each unfinished block. Soaring further,
We perceive the gaunt ribbing of mountains,
Eczema of clearances or the in-flight
Magazine; its articles on California
In England or the Turkish pavilion

At the Portuguese World Fair managing
To make everywhere a watered-down version
Of practically anywhere else. Out of the
Window again as the effortless river
Slips and slithers towards the horizon,
Writing a sunny italic with its unwound
Ribbon. The eye wades across plains,
Iris larger than lakes, penny-black forests,
Ravine cicatrices and the nervous system
For some rapidly fading anatomy where
Windscreens twinkle like vitamins. Tufts
Burst into puffs, herding above their own
Images; drifts, studies in floss
For the International Cloud Atlas.
Here is the scud of sailors, mackerel sky;
Clouds of radiation or of interfret,
Of inversion or of inclination:
Underneath, like beaches at low tide,
Herring-bone ridges, trickles and creases
Where shadow sea-horses wash among
Fleurs de lys. Clods of ploughed cloud.
Curl-cloud, stacken-cloud, fall and
Sonder-cloud; wain-cloud, twain-cloud
And rain-cloud. Through their clumps
Darts the minnow which passes our portholes:
We are to them as small as this to us.

3

At a slight angle, after stopovers too brief
To adjust the watch to, bisected by the aisle,
As in an airline model, we have flown over
The latest wolf-child with fingernails fully
As long as a secretary to a multinational
Who switches planes at Bangkok as metropolitans
Change their tube. Seat rows alter tack
As knees lock, necks crick and backs ache.
Uniforms lean over us: the world tilts,
Views are lost, clouds shrink, seats recline.
Dawn remains dawn or twilight begins again,
But llamas are being paraded up and down;
Fierce competition for stewards and hostesses
– Particularly for stewards with impossible
To bypass drinks vehicles. When the wing
Dips sharply manikins roll with the slope:
Men snore, engines drone, time grudges an inch.
The llamas smell rather, and spit. Despite
Everything the crew have maintained their poise
On the poops of the deck, at the announcement
From the captain, though a number of heads
Fall off fitfully into their neighbour's laps.
Throughout the cabin vines appear to sprout
Bunches and tendrils, and the plane drops
Into air-pockets with an upsetting of coffees.
Dreaming awhile is bliss, far away but dreadfully
Creasing the book at one's side. Is this
The interior of a majestic seaplane gently

Rocking on floats in a tropical harbour?
No, it is not. Remorseless babies awake.
Lights go dim except for the cockpit's
Constellation of dials below the night
– Inner sanctum with more stops than an organ,
Routing our flight-path by the stars above
Or beside us; responsible for all babies
On baby-racks below film-screens up the front:
They are commencing the long, gradual climb
Never quite managed out of childhood,
While all of Java teems below my aquavit.

4

I have done a few knee-jerks and again
Changed socks. Off come jacket and tie
As hot jets launch us down the wrong end
Of a telescope. From Paris to Manila
Via Jakarta, will we notice a few national
Characteristics in the physiognomy of our crew,
Garb of fellow passengers or complexion
Of cleansing personnel at obscure touch-downs,
Or land at the usual, endure the usual
And stuff down the usual at the very same
Fast food take-away service buffet
We queued at several thousand miles back?
Old land-locked communities are traded in
For transit lounges, concertina passageways
And adjacent antipathies, where Seventh Day
Adventists and Rajneesh promoters rub shoulders

With ayatollahs flying out to address
The faithful in a far-flung country town,
A remote atoll or a larva-riddled metropolis.
Dingy, unromantic travel, taking age-long
Minutes for its hop across a continent
Worthy of a lifetime's journey on a camel.
Shuttle-takers beat the rush by air:
Below them leopards cough, atrocities go off,
Popes wave to masses. Cramped by a window,
Baggage under the seat or stowed above
His head, a singer hidden by headphones
Does a flit from whoever wants him to
Become an accountant. The fledgling jet-
Setter whose tights itch will be met
By her introduction to heroin and the game.
At present both are insulated from fact
By cloudpacks afloat on incarnadine light.
There's only vapour underneath the immigrant
Whose trousers are too short; aether
Above his impedimenta of locks and skull-cap.
Earth's curve drops away from turban and fez,
Or rises much too swiftly to indemnify
A lack of the language in the new country.

5

Our young singer has mislaid his shoes
At the last festival of international noise.
I have mislaid my shoes, my antihistamine,
And expect trouble coming down next to the

Aunt whose youth was blighted by her acne
Sitting upright in anticipation of a reunion
With a family she does not know very well.
Next along, the director running downhill
In front of his steam-roller loosens a belt
Which is equivalent to letting hair down.
Sun or moon or stars give constant light
Far from what we can do anything about;
Flying to Paradise out of middle age, between
Old country and antipodes, from one predicament
Into another winter, from alp onto prairie,
From next year to a day before yesterday,
Breakfasting in summer – with a few hijacks,
Doubts, regrets, lonely dinners on trays,
Fresh loves and divorces going backwards
Or forwards into a different time or place,
Made a bit more haggard and more desiccated by
Inevitable views of porthole, wing and sky.
Sometimes a mountain edges its ridge into sight
As another flying McDonald's passes overhead
Pushing its cigar-tube through serene azure:
Those for whom here is nearly over there
Contemplate that blue in flushing toilets.
Going like turbines, gents eye nylons
Up to where they disappear: from there on
They have to use radar. Others con a movie
About test-pilots, airports or spy-planes.
Meanwhile, with alert, regular gyrations,
A bulldozer or ploughshare for sky sweeping
Turns through itself at the end of our route.

Minuscule Meccano bowls poke up at those
Who swallow their ears or writhe with a
Pressure headache, doze, dreaming of fishes,
Or administer the final, crucial touches
To their down-to-earth poems above the clouds.

6

Now an infinitesimal incline produces
Needles and vents in the pinions as we go
Bumpily from enlargement to enlargement;
The wing blenching, flickering through gaps
In appearances, obscurity of cloud stuff:
Citadels, ogres, winged horses pedestalled
On froth revealing a sombre underside,
With shallower sky beneath their turbulence:
Overcast details of suburban development
Seen through parts of the aeroplane shifting
Apart over a multiplicity of backgrounds:
Tennis courts, potting sheds, pools and hoists
At a miniature railway level just before
We bump against the runway, fighting back
An impulse to continue over the horizon.
Each comes to land with his adjustable
Upholstery, head-linen, buttons in the arm,
Headset and radio thumb-wheel, personal
Reading light, ashtray, ventilation nozzle.
Veteran of check-ins, lift-offs and air-lanes,
His God is the oxygen mask he takes
On trust above his head or the life-belt

Under his seat. Side-slipping eagle,
Out of the blue, he alights among carparks,
Semi-double-deckers, fork-lift trucks,
Corrugated fences and the tails of jumbos,
To rectal examinations, refusals to grant visas.
Back full of stories of tractors, lorries
In bags, a trolley and schnapps, there's Mummy,
His familiar shoulder. Will it eat the tails
Off aeros, the monster, the helical scan?
Cars pour into the long tunnel beneath
The airport like a postcard of a long tunnel
Beneath a different airport, as a DC10
Slides up the runway. He is a nice monster.
He could not carry on a clandestine affair
And be happy. The jelly will only be yours
If you eat more of your main course,
Or cross a detector's threshold ever to roam.

Motorway Miniatures

1

Another motor drifts into the jam
Edging across that major ring
Around the suburbs. Fingers drum
On the wheel: they belong
To the man whose girl nestles
Into her scarf, her coat too thin
For the weather which bustles
The clouds along. Cold air blows in
Through the boosted heater still,
If warming up with each new mile.

2

Outward bound, the flyover leans
Away from town. Her delicate hands
Feeling the chill, she wedges them
Between her thighs to get them warm;
Bundling his herring-bone overcoat
Into a ball to pillow her head.

3

As garden city gives way to factory
Meadow, vintage motorway bridges
Disappear behind trucks and taverns.
Out of a steep embankment hiding
A view of anything but the road
Ploughing the sheerest furrow through
Chalk beneath the brow of a hill,
Ample lanes come bowling down the swell
Into a patchwork trough of fields.

4

Wonderful power-lines fasten the cloudy
Parcels above them. They march in
Avenues across country, looping
A deliberate route across another set
Of themselves: their saucers that hang
Grandly festoon the arable scene.

5

As if by some unspoken agreement
On this stretch, several thousand cars
Travel in the same direction or its
Opposite. Either way, the accompaniment
Is wound past them onto a canister

Of gone forever: hill forts, damp
Looking fields, cattle stalls, barns
And dark plantations, parked feed
Barrows and sack trucks, concrete lots,
Blokes covering ricks and stacks in
Sheet polythene weighted down with tyres,
Or lining and sealing silage clamps.

6

Sights prove emblematic, noticed once
In name only, under a welter
Of directional symbols, videogame
Versions of the highway code:
We move the scenery. You relax
Or blame the projection – front and back,
It's screened from the Odeon's box,
Or so it seems, in paltry helter-skelter.

7

Then from a carriageway floating
Over some town-spilt plain,
She sees each slip-road circling
Underpass pillars into a warren
Of dwellings for cars, tunnels for broad-
Bottomed shoppers to amble its mall.
And lifted off the land, skirting the base
Of a silo, she feels as if she went
In a stream of ants across a table.

8

Wafted feathers fill the sky
From the corner of cloud
Bearing down on the road.
In a most leisurely way
Their finger-prints melt
On the screen as they land;
While odd patches of ground
Get tippexed to a fault.

9

Snow pink goose feather breast:
The marble buttocks on a bed of farms;
The major road wending its soft way
Through cleavages in sunset, satin
Tatters and scarlet. Travelling into
A drawing, the couple encounter
The silence of gulls blown inland
Among pigeons with their windows up,
The litmus paper sky, the truck
Going slowly over a blancmange hill.

10

The sun sets. The ego shrinks.
Ice-deposits collect around axles,
And lights look reflected off combos
Or drum-kits when it isn't sleet

Shivering over the deserted rest-spot,
The trim lawn, newly planted saplings,
The odd picnic and the occasional revolver
Talked about on the news. Twilight's
Careering succession of silhouettes
Makes shapes enlarging rapidly then gone.

11

To snatch a bite at a foul stop
They step across the sandwich spread
Of puke on the stairs, dodging a blitz
Full blast through stiff swing-doors.
'Try the curd. I'm going to the gents!'

12

Defeated though by enigmatic flush,
He retreats to ack-ack, the sonic clash
From plastic dial and screen set to go.
With door slam, they get started again;
Fastening themselves under strait belts
As he twists the key. They back
Out of a marked space, changing
Gear through bald spellings of fuel,
To cruise the first available pump.

13

When the pressure fails its trigger
With a clunk, he picks his way
Through slush to pay the attendant.
Next they slip into the slipstream
And away, keeping awake while driving
Through traffic in winter at night.

14

On into the dark travels the stream
Of red pomegranate seeds pairing off
In their direction. Flashing beams
Of glare splash more lemon after-
Image on their retinas. Ahead,
The cells drift toward the heart
Pulsating somewhere beyond the skyline.
Ears pop, nose dries up, and again
The screen gets sprayed with slush.
Touch the wipers, not too much.

15

Some have style; aerial, glider-like
Structures. They scud like water-
Boatmen over a pond across his screen,
Even at sixty through sludge.
It queers his twentieth-century trance

To have to jab at them every so
Often; works on the nerves when
Too few flakes fall from the night.

16

He gives the girl a glance;
Her head asleep on his coat
Against the window by the passenger
Seat while he persists, or
Him asleep on his coat while
She persists till the services
After next, mesmerised by bright
Approaches while she drives.

17

He dozes in the stream, fitful
On a wind that drags behind lorries:
Icy wet, their tarpaulins flap
Through sleepy visions of the bush
Of roads, of her bush, of an espalier
With branches, forks and twigs
Conducting traffic. Then with a blast
Of the horn, spraying his dreams
With muck, somebody big overtakes
On the inside carrying a dozen
Combines – a two-tier flat-bed truck.

18

Swipe, squeak go the wipers
As she leans forward to check
In the nearside wing-mirror.
Once he twisted an arm off
With a wrench. He screwed the arm
Back on. It still didn't work.

19

They stick with the drive, as with
A book which is a must to read,
It does help to remove the shoes,
Ease off swelling feet, hum a
Tune with the brain: you can't
Go home, you can't go home again.

20

Keeping awake, keeping awake
While driving through traffic
In winter at night, by gritting
The teeth, rubbing the neck,
Rotating the head when it jolts
Off to sleep on the shoulders;
Willing the eyeballs from rolling
Back, longing for blankets
And the hum without questions
Asked of a vital machine.

21

Involuntary resources control
The lungs' intake, the heart-beat;
Remote, automatic pilots
Take over from the commercial
Traveller, the old trouper,
With girlfriend or girl on the razzle
In tow, as the dipped lights
Lurch over a bit of landscape.

22

Knackered, they coast into dawn
At the next glass palace but one
On board a bridge. People who never
Meet in the same place again
Are seen in a bad light over coffee.

23

Not to be stared at in the wash
And brush-up, bare to the paunch,
His vest and shirt dangling from
A truckie's belt; overweight
Buddha of the late-night sauna,
Using his belly-flop to evacuate
The plunge pool by displacement.
Now he makes do with a sink.

24

Back across the stable table
It's real eye-shadow, and the skin
Blotchy, cracked around lips
And nostril rashes: looks dreadful
To him anyway, looking as bad
Himself on a cough and a sniffle
When they continue with tissue
After tissue stuffed behind
The heater vent above the dash.

25

Traffic-light coloured pastilles
Powdered with icing in a circular
Tin. Mini-slabs of barley-sugar
Neatly wrapped in silver paper.
These contribute to the litter
Mixed with receipts he remembered
To keep – odd coins, old bags beneath
And between her shoes and his feet.

26

Squeak, swipe go the wipers in an arc,
Lowering two half-moons to reveal
The back of the next container along
The queue he intends to overtake

As the wind-blown powder skitters
Like a wave along a beach across
The dirty road already nose to tail.

27

Would they say where they are going
Or care if it's there the rainbow ends
With bells on her toes whenever she goes
Past the shifting, whispering sands?

28

What is she doing here? In one lacuna
Between leaving and getting there at last,
She sits in the stationary car, a standby
For a place on the ferry from some port,
As he stretches his legs, forced to accept
The fact of a two-hour halt at the docks;
Wryly aware of his presence in a spot
That's only to be passed through on the way.

Boxing the Cleveland

A coach-built lorry, several metres long,
Is backing down the grass-bound lane between
The weather-boarded shack where clothes are hung
And that old shed for wood. The lane leads on

Past chicken-runs behind a criss-cross fence
On the woodshed side, beyond the much-decayed
Remains of a kennel, overgrown with dense
Nettles and docks, and then on past those frayed

Rails the horses gnaw through the winter, bordering
The sunset paddock, there on the laundry side.
The lane is closed by a new gate worth the ordering
With its lightweight bars on which the children ride

At the downhill end, and by one painted white,
Which is seldom used but can be pulled across
At the end where the ground increases in height
Towards those sheds behind the red-brick house.

The lorry's box is partitioned for at least
Four horses standing sideways in their stalls:
Its width permits a squeezing space at best
Between its sides and the nettle-bordered walls

Hard by the lane, where it's brought to a juddering stop
Beside the gate pushed back against the shed
Serving as laundry. Someone thin on top
Comes out of the house and greets with nod of head

The woman who switches the engine off, a breaker
Aged about thirty, dressed in jodhpurs, who lands
On the ground while a girl and a woman like her
Climb from the passenger side – her helping hands.

The three squeeze past the gate-posts into the lane;
Then rattles, thuds and hammer-blows are heard
As round the back the ramp is lowered, then
Its side-gates and its uprights get secured,

And a well-stuffed hay-net's hung inside the stall
At the ramp's head there, in readiness for the horse.
Quick swallows flit the sheds. It's early still
On a summer's evening. Horses crop the grass

Below a sky of livid, swirling veils
Auguring storms. The atmosphere is close.
The breaker woman clambers through the rails,
And in between the thistle-clumps she goes,

Holding a lunge. She's back inside a minute,
Leading a four-year-old, prancing, tossing his head
In its halter, fretfully stalling and fighting agin it,
But out of the sunset firmly and forcefully led.

44

There's a fine horse: a colossal Cleveland Bay
Bearing aloft his Roman nose, his ears
Pricked forwards as he strides, then sidles shy
Of an elder bush. He snorts now, as he nears

The horse-box, ill-disposed to walk in hand.
Unshod, as yet unbroken, how he towers
Above the woman eager to command
Obedience, however many hours

It takes to do it. Now she lays her stick
Against his neck and pulls him while his shank
Precedes the older woman who will flick
His quarters should he baulk, and at his flank

A smallish man in mackintosh and cap:
Together with the girl who shakes the pail,
This makes a team resolved he will go up
Inside the box – determined not to fail –

While he who came directly from the house
Decides to watch the struggle, not engage
In any sort of help beyond advice,
Or that is how he sees it at this stage.

At first the Cleveland halts to sniff the ramp;
The second time he brings a hoof to pound it,
Striking more than once to test his stamp,
And blowing dirt, his large head firmly grounded.

The woman breaker hauls him up again,
While those behind him offer him no leisure:
Pushing, prodding, beating him between
Hocks and haunches, they increase the pressure.

'Just keep niggling with the whip, Jane,
Rather than waving it wildly like that. Go on,
Go on,' the woman says. She tugs the rein,
Her hands in gloves to guard against a burn.

'Come on, Sweetheart, it'll be nicer in here:
No flies.' The flies outside enjoy the sweat
Of brute and human; crawl within each ear,
Or else beneath his loins – they make him fret

And whisk his tail. A shudder shakes his frame.
'Isn't the slope too steep for him, Miranda?'
Her looker-on has never caught her name.
Only a fool spectator would demand her

Answer. 'Lead him from a distance to it.
That way he approaches straight, Miranda.
Mind you, if he doesn't want to do it
That'll be that – one never can command a

Horse that big by sheer brute force.' 'He can't
Be given the chance of going back,' she says.
'But he's in a panic.' My God, what an aunt
Of a man to one who knows her Cleveland Bays.

'He's not in a panic. Why should he be?' she smiles.
'He's stubborn, so we'll cut him down to size.'
Of course the ramp is far too steep for heels.
But will the woman listen to advice?

'You'll never fight him up the ramp, Miranda.'
'My name's Virginia – and I'll get him there.'
Why should she give up? Her motto is never surrender.
With burning ears, the man might now retire

But stays to help. 'Good boy, that's right, good man!
Let's place his off-forehoof against the ramp
– Don't try to lift it, push him off it, then
He'll use the other foot, but watch his jump.

Come on, Petrushka! Rattle the nuts at him, Mary.
Don't let him have them – not until he's in.
Haven't we got any real nuts in the lorry
Other than grass-nuts? Mary, try the bin.

Hoi, you, don't push at me! How dare
You barge like that?' She whacks him on the jaw.
Changing her tactics, should he stand and stare,
She bullies him, or coaxes as before:

'There's a good horse! Try lifting his foot again.'
The smaller man encourages his wary
Movement forwards, punishing him when
His hooves recant – for being so contrary.

Fond words, and a thrashing when they fail:
The ramp becomes that terror of the brink.
Lead a horse to water, shake the pail,
But can you get him boxed or make him drink?

'Get behind him, Jane, it's just no use
Slashing at him from the front like that:
It makes him more determined to refuse.
Upset him, and we could be here all night.'

By now she can expect to pull him round
Back to the ramp's edge if and when she pleases;
Even force his forefeet off the ground
Onto the ramp – but this is where he freezes.

The trouble is the lane: its downward cant
Is yet another factor for each hoof
To cope with: since the ramp is at a slant,
This incline makes it steeper than a roof.

And what about the box? Of poor design,
That gap between its ramp-hinge and its floor
Creates a step – eight inches, maybe nine –
And here's a horse who's not been boxed before;

A gangling sixteen hands with much to learn;
Who jibs against the rein with lengthened neck
And drags behind. At grass since he was born,
He's yet to feel a saddle touch his back.

As darkness falls, the towering sky releases
Spatterings of rain by fits and starts:
The risk of slipping down the ramp increases.
Buttocks bared, the Cleveland stales and farts

Whenever half-way up it, looking stilted:
Leaning from his stubborn rear, he stretches,
Craning his neck out; whiffles at the tilted
Surface with his lips and nostrils, reaches

Forwards for that tantalising pail
Of pony nuts, and rising 'on his toes'
He teeters off his haunches – can he fail
To reach the treat one inch before his nose?

A hindhoof rests on edge – he's not prepared
To place it on the ramp though: once or twice
He's put it there before – but now he's scared
Of slipping on its rubber mat, because

Whenever he puts weight on it, the hoof
Slides from beneath him. Were he just to walk
Straight up the ramp collected he'd be safe,
But at full stretch, on rubber, with his bulk

Above his forelegs, forward moving these
More often than his stern, he comes unstuck
And flounders badly, stumbles to his knees,
To scramble his reversal, bruise a hock

Against an edge and yank his hapless breaker
Out of the box now, fighting to maintain
Her grip on him. And when he fails to make her
Let him go, he drags her down the lane,

Wrenching her elbows; scattering all as he battles,
Hauling her after him headlong into the bush
There by the woodshed, through those vicious nettles,
In a back-off only halted by the mesh

Which fences in the chicken-runs, and then
Bouncing his rear against it, blowing hard.
The woman pulls his muzzle round again,
But now he can't be got within a yard

Of where the ramp comes down across the lane
Without a good hard slash to sting his arse
Back into action – 'Keep him moving, Jane.
You're going to learn who's boss, you bloody horse.

I don't care if we're here till four o'clock
Tomorrow morning.' 'Come on, come on, ay,'
The flat-capped fellow coaxes, as they rock
The horse's quarters forwards. 'That's the way.'

'I want it set up so he can't reverse,'
The breaker says. 'Try bringing both the whips
Behind him now.' No better, if no worse,
He gets so far, and then he locks his hips.

'Try Push-me-pull-you: while I pull, you push.
Get your head up, get it up, d'you hear?
Do you, do you?' Giving him a bash,
Virginia is at pains to make it clear

The fight is far from over. All the same,
She says inside her shirt she's sopping wet
And grins at that – a lather-making game
For horses too though, judging by his coat.

The man with thinning hair attempts to put
His shoe-cap through the ramp-foot's metal ring –
One of the pair on which it's meant to sit
But rides askew on, causing quite a bang

Whenever she walks up it, horse in tow.
By bearing down one keeps the ramp-edge flush
With what's beneath it. There, it's better now;
No bang to send him backwards in a rush.

This makes an ounce of difference to initial
Moments, as the Cleveland follows on:
But such improvement soon looks superficial.
He will not go beyond where he has gone.

'I'm sure it's far too steep.' 'It isn't though,'
The woman says, 'He's just determined not to.'
(Why should she heed a man who doesn't know?)
'He'll do it, now he's got to where he's got to.

What happens here could prove the most significant
Event in all his breaking,' she insists.
'With proper schooling he could be magnificent,
But he'll be useless if he once resists

And finds he has the strength to get away with it.
He has to learn it isn't all in fun.
I tell you now, to wait another day with it
Would set him back. I mean to get it done.'

And now the other horses take to galloping
About the paddock, spinning him around.
'Do that again, I'll give you such a walloping
You won't forget it! Please don't walk around

Him while he's on the ramp. It just distracts
From what we're trying to do.' The breaker vents
Her spleen on someone watching who reacts
By keeping still behind a distant fence.

'Let's keep trying. Can you bear it? Good.
Petrushka, you come in, don't toss your mane.
The world could be your oyster if you would.'
How poached the ground along the darkened lane.

He's laced in froth, the woman hot and dirty,
Yet relentless; not a single break
From ten-to-six till past eleven-thirty:
A glass of water all she cares to take.

Tempted, wheedled, bullied, given stick,
That horse remains as bloody-minded now
As when they started – rearing up and back
Before the sky; a threat to those below,

His forefeet scrape the clouds, he topples over on
His haunches, crashes down against the rail,
The ramp-gates or the nettles or the chicken-run,
And rears afresh – takes all the rein – to flail

For balance, but he loses it and sprawls
Across the ramp, then rolls right through the bush;
And far too green to know quite how one falls,
He thrashes on his back like any fish

Flung gasping on the bank. He hates the line.
Again he rears, and now the lunge-rein snaps,
Or else he wheels and knocks the woman down,
And as she falls each flustered chicken flaps

And squawks behind the fence. He gallops over her
With hooves aflurry through the battered nettles:
Curled with covered ears, what hardly bothers her
Except for stings most certainly unsettles

Those who help. She rises to her feet
Before the others reach her. Someone goes
To hold the tossing horse. 'Are you alright?'
At least Petrushka keeps her on her toes.

The flat-capped man removes his mac;
The woman with the whip is losing heart;
The rattling of pony nuts goes slack;
But the nettle-prickled breaker wants to start

That Cleveland up the ramp again, although
Her jodhpurs have been stained from where he churned
Her briefly in the stingers. As from now,
He'll do it in a bridle – as she warned

The owner he might have to, since the halter
Will not hold him. Sheer determination
Gets the head-piece done without a falter,
Then he flings his head in consternation

Out of reach and shakes it. Most unsure,
He pauses near the lower gate to dung.
She manages to grab him by the jaw
And slip the snaffle-bit across his tongue.

She then secures the cheek-piece to its ring,
Fastens up the throat-lash, and he's ready.
Right away, it's far less work to bring
Him back towards the ramp. 'Now keep it steady.'

Things go better. Never by enough
To get him up the incline, home and dry.
'I'll take a cigarette. My word, he's rough,'
The smaller man says. Then once more they try

To shift his shoulders, bend him at the knee
And place his hoof some distance up the ramp.
'Take care he don't come down on you,' says he. '
'Cause if he did he'd land a fair old bump.'

And later, with the only light one dim
Effulgence from the box, before the chap
With thinning hair can quite manoeuvre him
Another step, and thus prevent a slip

By hauling him across the rubber mat,
And making certain that his hoof is brought
In contact with an elevated slat
To give him purchase, should he bring his weight

To bear upon it, up he goes, and down
He crashes on the man who promptly buckles,
Trapped beneath his girth, and duly thrown
Against the gate to smart among the prickles.

The smaller fellow pushes back his cap:
'If you reversed the lorry, so's the ramp
Fell open down the slope, we'd get him up.
He'd find it all downhill, and then the chump

Would feel as he was walking back towards
The other horses; now he must presume
He's leaving them behind. In other words,
We'd get him if he wasn't leaving home.

And if we close the upper gate as well,
And park the box just several paces, say,
Along the lane and very near the wall,
He wouldn't have the space to pull away.'

A dozen times already, that big horse
Has bolted from his handlers down the lane,
Has left them sitting straddled there to curse
The nettles, or he's torn away the rein

And galloped off towards his native premises,
To stand and toss his head above the gate;
Only to be brought back to his Nemesis
Beneath the moon, behind a four-horse crate.

Virginia is his Atropos. 'Don't think
You can just stand there, old son,' she says, giving
The rein a yank if he pauses too long at the brink
Of the ramp. 'Till you're in, life's not worth living.

Push-me-pull-you again, Jane. Up you come.'
And again the Cleveland slashes down at the ramp
With an unshod hoof to clang the slats and drum
The rubber mat there, shining smooth and damp.

'Get your head up, get it up, you brute!'
The strain begins to show – his one desire
To end it all, to fold away his feet.
No longer can the pony nuts inspire

An edging forwards; only fear of hurt,
When those who grit their teeth increase the force
Of their persuasions, brings him back alert,
Eyes rolling, ears laid back: a nervous horse

Out of whose foam-flecked mouth the bit will slide
When pulled upon, and though he loathes the thing,
And shakes his bridled head from side to side,
That bar of steel remains beside his tongue

And pulls him wheresoever she sees fit.
He follows willy-nilly – till she brings
Him near the ramp. She loosens off the bit
To double-pass her lunge-rein through the rings

And get a surer purchase on his head.
But even so, misgivings make him baulk.
There comes a time when one will not be led,
And further up the ramp he will not walk,

Although it grieves his tongue to so recoil.
He droops, his jaw agape, his weary length
Stretched out and up the ramp, resolved to fail,
With heaving sides, and hardly any strength

To carry on the struggle. Swollen pink,
His aching tongue lolls out between his lips.
With flattened ears, he stands in utter funk
Below the woman. Desultory drops

Are falling now. The one who's going bald
Suggests they put a carpet down below
His hooves to make the incline more a slide;
And while Virginia likes to run the show,

She doesn't take much urging to endorse
A paint-stained piece of carpet for its floor;
But this strange item only fills the horse
With more distrust, he backs away the more

And backs away again. To keep him calm,
They lay aside the carpet till at least
He has his forelegs squarely on the climb,
And then they spread the carpet out as best

They can beneath his belly, where it can't
Be seen by him, though offering a sound
Foundation should he trust the upward slant
To trepidatious heels and quit the ground.

Virginia makes a noise by sucking air
Through puckered lips, as if she begged a kiss.
'Get in there,' says the man with thinning hair,
His shoulder to the horse's quarters. This

Is never going to budge him, so the whip
Is used to loop a line behind his tail
Which is tightened while the fellow in the cap
Lifts a fetlock to that rattle from the pail.

But nothing works. They might as well try out
The change suggested by that smaller man:
The lorry's driven forwards and about
The turning circle, then towards the lane.

The Cleveland ambles past, perhaps in hope
That this ordeal is over, it's so late;
But now the lorry faces down the slope,
A yard or so beyond the upper gate.

Then once again the ramp is rattled down
And fitted with its uprights as before.
Again the horse is brought inside the lane,
The white gate swinging shut behind his rear.

It's after ten, and very dark by now
– The only light that feeble glow inside
The box, although the stars put on a show
Of pricked-out constellations where they ride

Between the fewer clouds. The balding man
Walks over to the cars parked cheek by jowl
Beside the barn. He gets into his own
And starts the engine. Once he hears it growl,

He flicks the beams undipped, reverses clear,
Then gently rolls towards the upper gate.
His head-lamps give the light which they require:
Twin incandescent discs illuminate

The horse's rump, the jodhpurs and the rein,
The girl who shakes her pail within the tall
Entrance to the box, the flat-capped man,
The woman with her whip, the waiting stall,

And then the hay-net, hanging from its hook
Untouched as yet. Partitions open wide,
In order that the naive horse may look
Beyond the stall and sense the depth inside.

The man who runs his motor feels content
To contemplate their progress from his wheel.
But soon it proves unpleasant to prevent
Obscurity – his engine starts to smell;

And if he switches off but leaves the lights on
He'll never get the car to start again.
It really makes no difference if she fights on
In the darkness, says the woman at the rein.

He kills the headlamps; goes inside to eat.
And by the time he wanders back to check,
The boxing of the Cleveland is complete.
He's feeding, while the women pat his neck

Inside his stall. He gets a good rub-down.
The ramp is raised. Virginia climbs aboard
And backs the lorry through the gate, to turn
And drive away with scarce another word.

Now that should be the end of that; however,
Late next afternoon both horse and box
Are back again: and it's as if they'd never
Been away. The breaker woman walks

Only with great difficulty though:
She had no problem getting home alright,
But then Petrushka did not care to go
Head first, descending, down into the night.

Instead, he felt decidedly installed,
And when she tried coercion, out he lashed
And caught her on the thigh, and so rebelled
Her stable girl got well and truly squashed.

So there he had to stay, since they were spent.
Tomorrow they would try a different tack.
But daylight failed to budge him, and he went
To some grand show beside her well-schooled hack

Who looked askance at one who never left
His stall to win a heat. Quite sans rosette,
He loitered in the lorry, though bereft
Of food and drink. He wasn't leaving yet.

The massive lorry faces down the hill
Inside the sunset paddock, opened wide
Among familiar horses: will he still
Refuse to take that necessary slide?

Out clatters he, his Roman nose held high,
No sooner than the ramp has touched the ground.
And ruefully the woman laughs to see
Him whisking his disdainful tail around

And striding off. But though he's got her foxed,
And though he gave her thigh-bone such a crack,
And though he strolls unbroken, he's been boxed
– And though he may not know it, she'll be back.

The Ballad of the Sands

She kicks off her shoes
As the season winds down.
It's cheaper on the rides,
But when she's got the blues
She usually decides
To go barefoot on the dune.

The Pelican Hotel
Boasts a good view of it
Looming over trees
Between swung swings
And children on the rungs
Of the amenities.

Trippers crack jokes,
Filling to the brim
Bins for their crisps
While balancing their smokes
On tables where the booze
Froths along its rim.

The moron on the patio
Cannot help but stare:
He leans against his minder
Afflicted with a glare
And seems to have arms
Where his legs ought to go.

To lug him or his friends
Up the steep sands,
The keeper at the gate
Loans toboggans at weekends,
Not that they accelerate
In anything but snow.

Here the sun intensifies
The tamarisk, and toe-grips
Collapse on a haunch.
The calm profile gets
Interrupted by silhouettes:
Each step setting off an avalanche.

The dune serves as prostitute
To loud sneakers now:
Hardly any foot
Of her without scuffed print.
Dogs, balls, men;
Jeans, bleached women –

They photograph toboggans
Which refuse to budge.
A dog's bark begins
To break the frail crust
Still intact, higher up
On the last ridge.

A sky swamped moon
Rises as the dune rises
Over plantations of pines.
The marram grass
Pierces her with sparse
Tufts poking up like spines.

Stiff, bleached marram,
Every plume and stalk
Shaking as the girl
Continues her solitary walk.
The bare feet fall
Without a sound.

The girl has no goal.
Savouring her wanderlust,
She brushes through the thickets
Inhabited by crickets
Till she wades the gust
Battling her skirt.

Her footprints are soon
Smoothed over by the wind
And you lose their descent
In some crater of the dune
Where the shade's crescent
Enlarges afternoon.

Boys shout bang from the ground.
But out of sight
Is clogged of sound,
And even further away
There is the sea, glittering
In stretches blurred by grey.

Flat-bottomed, bumbling
Cumuli address the coast:
Did the children pass her
At a run – tumbling
Because the steep
Impelled them all too fast?

Lower down, the dune
Gets caressed;
Losing all marks
Of upsets and mouthfuls of sand.
The breeze is the ghost of a hand
Moving over a breast.

A gnarled tree reaches
Under the skirts of a cloud
As you roam the beaches
And every tufted pass
Calling for the blue girl
Lost among the marram grass.

Orange berries glow
As the tamarisks encroach
On the dune: a slow
Drift of ripples
Volcanic in approach,
Or lava worn as a broach.

She might pick a spray
To set off her suit
As she makes her way
Through the streets to work.
Bushes of this sort
Deck the tiered court.

She wears dark tights,
And a tube skirt
Slit up the back.
Her high heels clack
Down the brick steps
By the lights.

Here the motors wait,
Easing off their brakes
And ready to accelerate
As others move across.
A sleek Rover overtakes
A double-decker bus.

Three flowered frocks
Get stranded on an island.
Someone dashes past
In a cardigan with mail
As a messenger locks
His bike to the rail.

Here the traffic
Trembles for the girl
Stepping out into it
As the lights change
And the wheels whirl
And she skips out of range.

Here the old Roman
Catches his reflection
As he glides past the bank
At the intersection
And swings round the taxi rank
In his dented Datsun.

Back in town again
After a day of triple lane,
Two direction curves,
Where the broken line
Altered sides from dip to rise
– A day full of swerves.

He drove on his own
Dazzled by the sun,
And his steering gave a groan
At each slow turn –
Groaned as in pain.
Back in town again:

A man who haunts
The venues of the young:
Lemur of his own youth,
Never mind the taunts
He may fling at himself,
On occasion staring at the truth.

Out of tune with his career,
This sham emperor
Cruises through the town
From sauna to singles bar,
Searching for some elixir
In a dented motor-car.

Pale old Roman:
He may be balding,
But he's no eagle, this one.
A hedonist at heart
With an outer shell
Which hasn't worn well.

Habitué of crowded pubs,
Connected by his eyes
To any parts in contact:
Brisk young thighs
Pushed against hips,
Reciprocating lips.

A surreptitious glance
And a half bitter smile
Establishes his stance;
A single man once more,
Answerable to no one,
What is he searching for?

The whiskey sour
In the right hotel
At the happy hour?
The attentive belle
Raised from the floor
At the end of her straw?

He is the attentive one
The lady in the navy suit
May notice drinking
At some adjacent table.
He's not that cute,
And she knows what he's thinking.

An hour later, therefore,
He seats himself gingerly
On a bench already wet
With condensation or
Some other person's sweat.
Sour steam surrounds him.

He soaks up the heat,
Tries to free his mind
Of its image of a girl
Observed on a dune
Battling the wind.
A girl like the moon.

She looked blue, beautiful.
But now his session's up.
He vacates the steam
As a blond, busty treat
In pale aertex freshens up
Each dank corner of the suite.

Here he is again,
Limper now, but clean,
Cruising through the streets
With stars in his sights
– Or are they just the lights
Reflected in his glasses?

Nice if he could score,
But he doesn't take
Enough care anyway.
The core of a pear
In his key-tray
Shouldn't be there.

Somewhere in the eighties
He lost the art of chatting up.
Getting laid is serious
For an unassuming chap
Saddled with the tastes
Of a Tiberius.

Absent-minded
When he's on the hunt,
He glides past the moon
In his Datsun saloon
With the dent at the back
And at the front.

He glides past the starred
Lugubrious hotel,
Where old turds gather
In the stair-well,
Queuing for the lecture
On the Bard.

He ought to be there,
Not heading for the disco
Along from the fair
At the far end of town,
Just up the shore
From the marram-covered dune.

The wenches go out there
In their Lycra underwear,
Soon to be upended
By the Zipper:
They shriek down chutes
And they wail on the Dipper.

The Cyclone Twist
Isn't to be missed,
But later on
They like to frisk
Around their bags
To the latest disk.

Chic teen dreams
Flicker in the beams
Of the syncopated spots
Till the fog-machine
Messes with their curls
And they join the other girls.

One of them has been
In trouble with the Law –
Not for nothin' serious, mind.
Call one a whore,
But the rest are amateurs,
Partially inclined.

And though she would rather
Be sampling the rides,
The one in the turquoise
Hiccups and confides
In the eager gentleman
Who could be her father.

She spits as she chatters,
Passionate and squiffy;
Pressing where it matters
And giving him a sniffy;
Boasting that she lifted
Her perfume from Boots.

Wonderful sensation
Of spittle on his cheek
Spat from such lips,
And he likes the reek
Of tobacco on her breath
As she slags off probation.

She hasn't done time,
And she's not on the game,
And she has a feller,
But they're all the same
– Young men at least:
They get you all creased.

With an older bloke though
A girl can depend
On a drink for herself
And one for her friend:
What matters at the disco
Is what you've got to spend.

You seat her in the dark
Of your comfortable saloon,
Slap in a cassette,
Turn the volume down
And take her to the car-park
Out by the dune.

Uncertain what she'll ask,
You offer her a swig
From your flask;
And then in lieu
Of further talk
You suggest a walk.

The big full moon
Diminishes the stars,
Hones every shadow
To a knife's edge.
A tree's dead spars
Appear dim though.

What is it moves
Out of the sand
In which it has sunk?
It's only a trunk.
Utter darkness
Rustles in the groves.

The moon shines bright
Between grey fleeces:
Her radiance increases
The bowl of the dune,
Felt as very large
Even in the light.

She slows down the cloud,
Blazes on the creatures
Sunk in their gloom.
Imperiously proud,
She travels by the light
Of her features.

Having spilt love,
You're too dazed to move;
And though you should be brisk
The moon numbs your feet,
Roots you to the spot
By the tamarisk:

The place off the track
Where she said
She'd had enough
And wanted to go back;
The place where you dug
The shallow trough.

She may not follow,
But you must get away
From the hollow
Where she started to shout.
Time is the sand,
And yours is running out.

Nothing shines so brightly
As the white ball of light
Bearing down from afar.
Prints remain visible
On this illuminated night.
You must get back to the car.

Melancholy hooting
Floats across the motionless
Ripples which cover
The flanks of the dune
You stumble over.
Dawn will come soon.

Next will come the minder
Who tugs the moron
Through the sandy places
In a hired toboggan,
With little else to do
But follow up your traces.

You are completely alone
With the dune and the moon:
Sufficiently high
To catch the lighthouse
Many miles away
Flashing once, then twice.

On this saddleback of sand
Gusts and eddies move
Her grains into a collar-bone;
A long, curved ridge
With a sharp edge above
The steep plunge down.

The pine plantations sough.
You are about to go down
Into a cleavage of time
Occluded by a cloud
Fashioned like a clown
Which is changing even now.

It has become the skull
Of some tormented girl,
Her mouth open wide.
The moon disturbs her mane,
Passes through the fringes
Of her brain.

She gets lost inside,
And the world goes dark
Before you get back
Through the pines
To the carpark.
Everything looks black.

But she sails through the cloud,
And her radiance comes back;
And the whole dune glints
And shimmers as you'd wish it,
If those damn prints
Didn't somehow blemish it.

Creakings in the pine trees.
You slip past the corpses
Of wart-hogs –
Or are they logs?
You just make the Datsun
But can't find the keys.

You can't have locked them in!
Not in the ignition!
Absent bloody minded
By your own admission,
Now you're stuck, blinded
By their dangling.

For in between the blackouts
Perpetrated by the clouds,
As a chill enshrouds
The car-park in silence,
The moon grows intense
And uses these to dazzle you.

A Walker on the Wall

The orange digger can be seen for many miles,
From many pastures and as many lanes,
And from this stationary if impermanent car
Parked where the stationing of caravans
Is forbidden, it can be seen disgorging loads.
But in between lie unrelated fields:
Attempting sedges battered by the tempest,
Trousers only dampen at the knees
When brought up sharp at each and every turn
By some canal with hawthorn at its edges.
No way to the sea-wall through these traps,
Unless by sluice-gates, half a mile away,
Or by the church, and that's at least a mile.
My chosen path must renounce its doctrine:
Best to walk away from where the digger sits
Biting on stone-chip, keeping all intact
Against the worst abrasions of the winter.
Back on the road, a lorry splashes past
With a rusted skip for further up the coast.
A heron floats off westwards, while the cows
Shelter by that double line of poplars
Bent above them, buffeted by squalls:
Pellets bounce off leaves, brims, eaves
And rims of things, while tatterdemalion veils
Get pasted onto the sky, making it whiter.
Willows churn like whirlpools on the boil
Or people surging frantic at some barrier.

The sea-wall is a break between two worlds:
Above the dead flat land it constitutes
The absolute horizon line behind
Whatever gets between it and the eye.
Being unable to reach it for a time,
Your view beyond is rendered hypothetical.
Is there a sea at all, is there a storm
On the far side of the wall? Is there a part
That is constantly turned away from us,
Completing us, the far side of our moon?
Walls exist to stop this getting into that,
Forbidding seepage, even through a straw.
You can say that he stonewalled or that she
Was just about as wall-eyed as a goat,
But meanwhile, above a works caravan,
A Water Board bulldozer and a bungalow,
The digger raises an arch between askew
Telephone poles and a bunker, reaches down
The incline, scooping to itself the heaps
Pushed at it by the bulldozer below.
And while the cabin spins to salt its load
Over the wide, flat top to the wall,
Garnishing its surface, flattening
The area with a heavy tooth, the weather
Keeps on flowing through the brakes,
Dribbling onto turquoise rows of kale
And tossing rushes clustered like bamboo.

These then are the fen-like Wentloog Flats
To which I come on Sundays off and on,
Sometimes with my son or with my friend.
The gypsies like it too: they use its sites
And often tether ponies to its verges.
Farms between the mountain and the marsh
Raise Dutch barns on lowlands to the north,
While all the south is given to the estuary.
For dike there is that ridge we call the wall:
A track for tractors runs along its top.
Beneath it moves a filth-tinctured stream
Invisibly, its vivid duckweed film
As stagnant as a moat's beneath a rampart.
Crisp-packs flutter gaily in the meadows
Criss-crossed by these ditches known as reens:
The coast roads run in tandem with their trenches,
Though no one can be certain which began this.
Broken, where the wall surveys the sea,
And left as flotsam shored against its mound,
Lie jerry-cans, the torn hoods off prams
And ruptured tires distorted by their scorching:
Tokens of some drowning on dry land,
The palsied earth itself being every jot
As frail, inconstant, waving as that blot
Beyond the Flats, its closer water slack
In the mud's runnels, isolating tussocks
Where the stakes diminish with the distance.

The tide is out a way. The plovers gleam
And paddle. Somewhere off these barrier stones
A peewit, then the trundling of a train
Faintly moving at speed across the land
As breeze-blown mares go ankle-deep to graze.
The rocks are piled where tides may rush at us,
Though nettles use their lea-sides with impunity.
Seabirds blot the freighters in the waterlane:
At long distance, people read as dots.
Every footstep starts pips and chortles;
Flocks of pipers fluttering suddenly upwards,
But no shooting where the cows lean
Up the grass bank, and the grey-winged gull
Gets nowhere against the wind but floats
Higher than reach. This is the wind that lifts
The long-feathered wings of the crow before it flaps.
Who knows what you may find on the road
To the watermark pole with its yellow band:
Desolate place of inner tubes and milk-crates;
Canisters rusted and devoid of gas;
Mud cracked all over its crust; tough
Grasses looking accustomed to being submerged.
A backlit sky from the moors at sunset
Beams up searchlight rays between ridges
Of cloud above the black tower of the church
North of the wall; and on its chancel's side
The flood is marked at chin-height by a plaque.

Sixteen-hundred-and-six had just begun:
A sad time, when to sit in a tree was a blessing
Close to a chicken. Others fared far worse
That January, as it pleaséd God,
When retribution rose up to this brass,
And in the rapid matter of the flood,
Without avail, this parish sadly lost
A good five thousand and an hundred pound,
Besides the twenty-two odd persons tossed
Out of their beds, and then completely drowned
With several thousand others in the parishes
Spoiled by the grievous fury of the sea:
Livestock confounded, hayricks whisked away,
And multitudes of buildings beaten down,
For no greyhound could have run before
The waters as they raced in on the houses.
Then the dead were swept away as well,
While Elphin's coastguards wallowed in carouses.
All the church lay drowned beneath its bell,
The wall in disrepair since Roman time.
And now the churchyard cannot raise a tomb,
For who would care to flounder in their shroud,
Or barge among comestibles and kine,
Brought horribly awake behind the coffin-lid?
Built, flooded, burnt and restored – it took
A fire to dry the rafters – usual history
For churches near a lighthouse on a marsh.

Now, in the yard, a horse bites at its crotch.
Goats bleat from a rainswept field nearby.
Blackberries dot the harried autumn hedges,
Peppered already with hips as well as hoars.
Ivy strives to strangle tangled brambles.
Docks clog the fosse. By Sluice Farm
A house of stone gets coated pebble-and-dash.
Limes pale. Barns accumulate haydrums.
Continually the thistles rub their frowzy heads
Against the hollow stalks, the ghost branches
Of the cow-parsley, while thin grasses
Whistle under concrete steps over the bridge
And up the wall from the caravan park.
Lanes led off the coast road finish here,
Or else at isolated farms, yards for stacked
And bashed-up cars glimpsed through barricades.
The rushes bluster just as much in summer
As in winter here: rushes dense as bamboo,
Good for murder. I can see that ferret
In his van curse because our damn Cortina
Dawdled down the road on some off-chance
A noticed track would take us to the lighthouse.
Once we walked there from the caravans
To find its lantern smashed to smithereens.
But what a staircase! Curving round the rail
In thirties style; and then there were the rooms
Like grapefruit-sectors, leading off its spine.

That architect we took some other time
Quite fancied you, and sat me in the back
Of his extremely small, unhappy car
– Unhappy when negotiating ruts.
We never made it though, the three of us:
His urban chassis couldn't take the muck,
For things get tricky underneath the wall,
Where nightingales may nest in cathode tubes.
I tell you, on a bend I saw a goose
Ruffling its feathers in a depot once.
Petals thrive on refuse at the sewage-farm.
Rabid vegetation spoils the ditch:
Summer long, it's wet for vetch and nettle.
Martins flick the tarmac near the boarded place.
They raid the cattle. Ponies stand with rears
Too near their fronts; manes slack with damp;
Tails each a wet rope. August storms
Come crashing down, dousing clanks from tractors,
Dampening sacks on rickety farm-trucks,
Tail-boards fastened with raffia. Hammering
Hardens its beat on the roof of the car:
What is straight goes zigzag down the screen.
Poplars hiss Medusas, breast a surge
Which seems to run full sail before the blast.
Water pours off the ribbed sheeting on barns
With every gust, while gulls driven inland
Feed off manure in fields smelling of pigs.

The sea-wall stands between this eerie fen
And marshes which in winter seem Siberian:
Tussocks frost, mud supports your weight;
Shallow reach turns dark, ice sheet,
And wall-walkers muffle up their ears,
The wind being cruelly keen above its edge.
They leave it then to stretch deserted on
Towards the town where men are just as sharp.
One fellow named a time and then a place;
Met her there, or so the judge was told,
Sealed their assignation with a kiss,
Then threw his pregnant woman off the bridge.
But who can blame the wall for what goes on
In disused sheds and alleys near the tracks?
That's beyond its precincts: it's the marsh
It draws its line across, between the towns,
Above the vacant cable-drums like magnified
Reels of cotton, rolled out on the strand:
Below the heavens, under nothing less
Except the steelworks at the river's mouth
Which contribute their vapour to the cumulus.
Having lived here now about a year,
I know the wall, or think I do, and stroll
For several miles on breezy afternoons
Before I meet a soul; though when my friend
Sketches a tree-trunk, up the tree-trunk gets,
Uncoupling the beast which has two backs.

Why do I walk when I can along the green
Ridge of the sea-wall, emphasised by light
Behind my silhouette, as I see others are?
I walk to find some motive, I suppose,
Choosing to plumb this radius of the sky
And scavenge meaning where the sea can barely
Be discerned – the tide has pulled it back
Behind the mud beyond the salty marsh.
Here there's a choice of east or west at least,
Where solid ground is kept from stuff less sure.
I walk at height above proposed alternatives:
Voyager's viscous, variable emoluments
Weighed against landlubber's property
Where the water moves in canals only.
Salt air or manure, you see me hesitate,
Then observe me mooch towards the marsh,
Kick at some sea-smooth twist of driftwood,
Climb the wall, descend towards the reen,
Attracted by some half-submerged contraption.
Veerings these, but not affiliations:
Torn between our countries and careers,
We still may walk, avoiding made-up minds,
Through sunny showers, the sky diverse in mood,
As if the weather wanted to agree with us.
Across the sea, the hillside fields are bright,
For faintly, after sheets of wet, the ghost
Of a rainbow glows and as swiftly fades.

When spring begins by tagging wool to briars,
After the stile, we run on up the steps
And quickly top this barrow of a wall
Immuring sod from shore. We pause for breath,
Descry the dead armchairs, fractured flower-pots.
No better time for poking through this jumble
Hand in hand. We pick our way past mattresses
And cowpats flies lift off on such a day,
Beneath a pale blue sky trailed by planes.
Here you can walk, and feel as if you ride,
Your head higher than the feed-hoppers on sheds.
Bedraggled calves concede the sea-wall track,
Maundering down its slope, crushing discarded
Egg-boxes as they go, blowing awry the teasels.
Should we thank the gypsies or the waves
For all the odd regurgitations tantamount
To wealth discovered here: the bibs and bobs
Attracting boys and magpies? Hard to say.
Only the skylarks act as if indifferent,
Babbling on, into the cauliflower ear
Of a passing cloud. Later we go by the reen,
Where the roan stallion with the white blaze,
Neat socks and flowing mane wrenches at a bush.
The boy uncovers an ants' nest under a stone.
He chucks the stone into duckweed – more of a plop
Than a splash – but enough to make the creature
Move off with a snort behind the hedge.

It's early for the tortoiseshell, I'd say,
Staggering past my nose upon the breeze,
Concerned with thistles pushing through upheavals
Demolition made when breaking up
Foundations left where something stood; the frame
Torn off its hinges sheds no light on what.
That old gate could do with some repair
Beside the solid crossing for the cattle
Tunnelled by its water-bearing pipe.
It's here the wall runs high across the land.
Cows recline like goddesses on top of it
And chew the cud as if it were our destiny.
Test-pilot ducks engage in flight,
Rolling at low level over Peterstone,
To land among the toppled, Gothic trunks
Of naked trees got-up as unhorsed knights.
Mild surf sounds their litany from afar,
While pathos dribbles from the weeping sluice
Which causes shivers where the film allows
A stretch of rusted water to reflect
The halves of footballs booted out of reach.
Are they balls, or ancient ball-cocks actually,
Abandoned when their cisterns failed to flush?
There is a place in the world then for the junked
Engineering of discharge, the jakes' graveyard,
Where even the porcelain for our waste products
Ends as a shard, fallen apart on the marshes.

Telephone poles and a bunker: this is where
The orange digger back in autumn went
Extending down the ridge to scoop itself
Stuff pushed at it by the bulldozer below.
After we round the watermark pole and decide
Enough is enough, the boy sees an exact
Replica of this machine, lying in the debris
On its side beneath us by the bungalow
Just where the real one mustered chips of stone.
This chance event is form devoid of sense:
Walking around for a year, you get to know
These incidentals conjuring coincidence
Which throw amusing patterns on the void.
Rusted but serviceable still, the toy
Thrown out to erode among those castors.
'Can we have this then?' I ask of the man
In overalls watching us while his Alsatian
Incessantly barks from within the fenced-in yard.
The man's head pulls in and then pokes out again.
'Sure the kid can have it.' What a find!
Past the teasels then, we saunter back,
The acquisition swinging from my hand
Or dangling from the shoulders of the boy.
But now we should hurry past the grey sheep
Sitting still as stones and cross the stile
To reach the coast road. From behind the church
Chimes can be heard from the van selling ice-cream.

Border Country

Whichever route we take, we lose the way:
After the trout-farm, for instance, when the lane
Keeps leading us along the valley floor
Until it hops the stream to climb a while,
Only to descend and re-negotiate
The maze of meadows in the stream's vicinity.
Winding on through alders, then avoiding
Pine and larch plantations, it continues
Dithering until it reaches Llanthony.
Here I doubt the road: it ought to climb,
Since I remember some amazing views;
And so reverse, to turn and then retrace
The single track till Cymyoy reappears,
Its tower askew by landslip or design,
Suggesting how a head should hang aslant
When hands are nailed – and *yoy* is Welsh for yoke.
Above the weathered hamlet which it serves,
The sliding mountain has a yoke-like look:
And where a yoke would dip to fit a neck
Monks on mules brought bitter through the gap
From Longtown which is just across the border.
However, this is not the time to stop:
When I reach the cross-roads, I go left,
Then left again, to crawl behind some ponies
Carrying a trekking party upwards:
Little girls with curls which do not fit
Their velvet-covered riding caps, with glasses
Bouncing on the bridges of their noses.

At the top of this steep stretch of hill
The tarmac peters out: we're forced to stop,
While the Black Mountains claim the riders.
Now we've got no option but to roll
Down the lane and take the route abandoned.
Right, then right again, and back we go
On tracks we just retraced, and then once more
Along the by-road following the stream,
Slowing at its bends, and backing up
For motorcades descending from the pass
Presumably some distance up ahead of us.
Flitting by a stand of twisted sycamores
We swerve to miss a pheasant, notice bulls
And buzzards, come again to Llanthony,
And pass the point beyond the Half Moon pub
At which I lost my nerve, with Offa's Dyke
Above us on the ridge which marks the border
Separating undulating Hereford
From the bald, escarping hills of Gwent.
Later, though, the blackest hill of all
Bulges at us through a perfect blaze
Of hawthorn blossom slashed at by the wipers.
Rising well above two thousand feet,
This knob is dubbed Lord Hereford's – the Tumpa.
It's a steep, uncompromising bump
Giving the impression of a camel:
Like it, lump it, there's no easy way
To scale the thing, and Dilys says at once,
Derek's mountain! Derek is a painter
Haunted by this gloomy shape: it stumps him
And looms up, an image in his mind

Often seen through such a blaze of hawthorn.
On we go though, since our guiding stream
Winds around it: then we start to climb
On and up and ultimately over
Gospel Pass, to meet the panorama
Taking in both Hereford and Powis
Laid out like one's crumpled bed at breakfast.
Ploughed fields, whale-backed hills, dingles
Moving into ever more be-misted
Visionary vales beyond the Wye
Looping round the bookshop town of Hay.
High above the larches, we are partly
Made of sky, we feel, as we look down:
As if we'd left the ground and joined the blue,
Or balanced on some line between the two.
And later, coming back from Hay, with loot
Sufficient for a bookstall in the boot,
We thunder briefly, as we cross the grid,
Ascending steeply, and encounter mist
Before we reach the ridge: its sluggish density
Has left a chilling trail, a slime of frost
On every mound of turf along its path.
Flakes of snow drift singly to the screen
And disappear. The whiteness keeps us mute.
Rushes mark where moisture leaves the slope,
Otherwise there's nothing to remark
Until the mist gets thinner, which it does
As we come down, to catch the lovely sight
Of many coloured hillsides brushed with snow
Which deepens as each brow begins to curve
Towards the cloud. Across the border now,

I can't believe how aimlessly we drive,
Having eaten well at Ross-on-Wye.
We don't know where we're going, do we though?
My mother can't remember which hotel
My uncle mentioned: something court or grange
Or manor even, in a place called Pen
Or Pen-something, somewhere close to Ross.
Bear in mind my uncle's name is Ross:
I get pretty vexed by our predicament.
When we draw our blank at somewhere grange
Some very kind hotelier intervenes
By phoning round and checking out all manner of
Manors, courts, and granges in the area.
Contact made, we sally forth again;
Speeding rather, plummeting down sleigh-runs
Shaped by veering hedges, missing trucks
Lurching at us by so many inches,
Turning minutes later, up a drive.
It leads us to a well-appointed, white
Facade above a golf-course on a slope
Which gradually declines towards a lake.
I'm vague about this, though, because it's raining
Hard when we arrive, and so we scurry
Up the steps and through the double doors
To come across my uncle in the lounge.
We press hands, brush each other's cheeks.
It's true that people shrink at getting old.
My uncle seemed an overbearing tree
When he stooped to let me know the intimate
Facts of life which I already knew
From witnessing how spotted dogs were mated.

He seems darker, shrivelled like a prune,
Or is it just the darkness of the rain?
We sit, though, and manage quite a chat.
He suffers from a squamous type of cancer
Which, he says, sounds to him like squeamish.
This affects the surface of his kidneys.
That's the way it crumbles, I am told.
My cousins now appear with many children:
Chocolate-fingered here, amid the sumptuous
Upholstery, they ruin conversation,
Hide behind the drapes or wander off:
And, simultaneously, my famous cousin,
Who's a tv star and runs a phone-in,
Seems to have mislaid the rubber eye-piece
Off his in-laws' 'steady-cam'. Disaster!
Helpfully I search beneath the skirted
Sofas for a while but can't retrieve it.
Gosh, the gardens here are simply lovely:
Roses climbing over bits of buttress.
How the children would have loved to play here,
Had it not been pouring, as is typical.
My uncle hankers after people though.
He has driven all the way from Crawley
To be here. And yet the children seem
Merely to provide my gilded cousin
With an interference which protects him
From the risk of deeper intimations.
My other cousin snaps when tea is served
And he's supposed to mind a pressing child.
I'm sure I like him all the more for that.
I want to go on chatting with my uncle:

It may be the last chance I get.
His wife says it's practically a miracle
That here he is recovered, almost well.
I don't know – he looks ill to me.
He's advised me many times – on property,
On girlfriends and divorces, and most recently
On my mad mother's passion for her builder.
Now he seems to occupy the border
Between life and death, or so I feel.
Cream tea is a bit much with six
Children in a rather grand hotel.

The Holiday

There's camping by a ladder to a roof-rack in the stars
On pine-scented avenues beside the heavy breather.
But everywhere we stop is a hazard for the radio,
So please shove it past your sword and underneath the seat.
The journey takes its toll in back-aches you can get
Massage-bead seat-covers for, in missed exits or
Slip-roads taken when we should have passed them.
Do we want all directions or simply some other direction?
Even one would do. I bought him the sword in a walled town.
Now he tries to riposte with it when technically
He ought to cut and thrust. He can use it on the thistles
Which infest the farm; but now it's to be put away
Since there are chores to be done: the rubbish hefted.
Evening brings a transient glow lit by canvas anterooms,
And crickets chirp to the fugitive hiss of camping-gas.
Then, as dew condenses on outer shell transparencies,
I spread my mat and wish the human motor had a choke.
Converted to my reconditioning mainly by the missionary
Position of my press-ups, I intend to overwhelm beholders:
Never were such flexed locations come across on me.
Dilys whips through her routine as I chivvy George
Zipped within his combat tent, asleep beside his sword.
Now the pinelight scumbles humble circumflexes
Back with their baguettes extruding from their bicycles.
Dilys sharpens her tools, but there isn't time to execute
Such quaintnesses. A fast crawl to the pool bar with
The underwater stools, and we must deconstruct ourselves.

Later, in a crowded cove, we get a shadeless pitch
Where the feeble pegs provided by our fabrications
Buckle when we try to make them penetrate the ground.
Here are tribal caravans with lobbies for their stoves,
And anti-insect neon casting flares of lumination
Over sisters, cousins, aunts and floors of pseudo-parquet.
We get away at dawn, exhausting this infringed-on coast
So fierce about its horns – so burdened by its bulevars of concrete:
Shorelines everywhere sacrificed to time-share;
Umbrella pines o'er svelte resorts irradiant from roundabouts.
Gentle dunes are overcome more easily by speculation
Than the perches crags provide for hermit millionaires.
On the flat-lands flats amass and floods of souvenirs!
Confining plants to *jardins* here eases plots for parlours
Manicuring smorgasbords; boutiques turned fish-and-chip shops.
Where can we erect our poles without a medical service?
Must we end on the nudist rocks frequented, says the guide,
By savage campers? Toilet bunting breezy on all ledges –
In the teeth of placards, posted by a conscientious few,
Beseeching stripped arrivistes to transport their ordures
Up to where binoculars ensure they get collected.
Best to drive bitterly on, towards remote advertisements,
Verandas falling back as we ascend abruptly now,
Though every corkscrew turn on this opportune promontory
May reveal another infestation of our kind.
In the last possible cove we find a site, and naturally
Morning finds me cranking up my corporeal engine:
Numberless dynamics keep me busy pumping things,
Then I jog with caution to the gym-club on the hill.
For sportive types they're softish, given a funicular
Elevates them to the showers after they have scuba'd.

See-thru flippers undulate a wasp swimsuit down below,
And signify the species with the triggerish harpoon.
Sub-aqua, we've evolved these webbed extensions to the toes,
But flapping on the rugged rocks who'd want to be a duck?
Underwater weeds wave like Disney at the shoals,
And you can reach among these eager minnows in a mask,
Scattering formations in an instant made of darts.
Beached ahead, the blissful Med just nibbles at the citadel
Praised by someone bare below the hammocks of her brassiere.
Cooler now, the post-siesta strand begins to thin,
With love's adherents clinging on as others start to fold:
They roll up and collapse, and, even as the dinghy teeters,
Key-rings tintinnabulate to flip-flops over sand.
Someone spanks a lilo as the lessening beach expands,
And Dilys stabs at lovely subjects resting napes in smalls
Of backs, and shaking when supports command departure.
People troop to the car-park carrying babes and baby-gear
Or winding bold chromatics about afflicted shoulders.
Every day the beach gets laid, and little girls 'veronica',
Though George the bull belittles any play for him.
He gets a butterfly-knife for his birthday – yet another blade
Collected for the sake of it – I never see him cut so much
As string. Every day we snorkel in that under-tent,
And foam clouds crevices of urchins or anemones
Where avatars in rubber come to trace the ghosts of fish.
Above the silver lining where their element begins,
Harried sand has granules more vermilion than the fellows
Lagering paellas in tavernas under blinds.
People split and wrinkle as the water comes together.
Someone takes apart a parasol as others beach
Their black pneumatic outboard with the single yellow stripe.

And at about this time, within a crimson ring of boards,
A yellow hose is dampening the sand while pasodobles
Rallentando right around the Tannoy. Trees beyond
Our seats extend their silhouettes across the killing-ground.
Nearly six o'clock now; and bussing in like us,
Tourists in extreme sombreros pat their loaded wallabies,
Or leap from place like crickets taking photos of themselves,
For the fans are now aflutter in the bull-club of Gerona,
And pennants flurry stripes at the crest of the arena,
As the hose is drawn in and late ones wedged in between
And flexed greys high-step rather lavishly and after
The parade we get the rakers and an orchestra
Ruptures wind haphazardly above a pride of matadors.
In comes the bull at a trot, breaking into charges and
Enlarging from the haunches, though like a barge to turn
When capes on offer swirl away the target for the horn.
They run at him with banderillas held flamenco high
Above his shoulders while he tilts quixotically at sails:
Easy to miss, and even if palpable, shaken loose by
An angry toss – who now stands stock still and black,
As the wasp-slim novice in his epaulets removes his cap,
Sweeps the lumbering rush beyond him, sucking ever thinner,
So the sharpness passes very close. And after that,
As the banderillas drain the apex of his back,
The bull begins to falter, and his killer knees the sand,
Showing the muleta with a debutant vulgarity.
A last rush is mustered, though the head nods in disarray –
The blade sighted, aimed, and shoved between the vertebrae,
The struck beast wafted in circles till he keels aside.
Then the mule-team brings the harness in, and as the fêted
User of the sword freshens up at the side of the ring,

The carcass is connected by its horns which serve as handles,
Dragged around the sand, then dismembered off the scene,
As eagles wheel and circle and continue circling in
A cloud above some natural arena made of crags
Where canine echoes bark inside the rock, or so it seems.
Effortless, their wings ascend, increasingly remote,
As George proceeds to bark back at the wilderness for fun
And small stones roll on our exit from this kettle-drum.
Then once more we pack ourselves as best we can between
Our sleeping-bags, inflatables, penknives, swords and pencils,
As we begin our climb towards the stations of the sun,
Identifying campsites on our longish journey home.

Dancers in Daylight

Paris, who the gods love, who desire slays;
Palaces on crater lips, ivy-covered trees.
Paris, and a cave with broken statuary.
Domitia hears how Dom gouged his head out.
Twisted gates, the mouth blocked by stone fall.
Here's the staved-in scallop of a swimming-pool:
A ripe place for chucking out your mattresses.
Paris, and an olive struck; well it might have been
Him in that track-suit, yearning for the West
Near those famous gardens uplifted over Rome.
I had been mooning on the Palatine since 10 am;
Sat at a sunlit banquet in the Flavian House,
Being Statius, looking up in awe
At rafters there no longer. I had traced
Domitian's maze. Could Q. Sulpicius Max
Have mastered its octagonal, commended at eleven
In the games for poets held in AD 94?

Gentle, perpetual anxiety of minor waves
Around the lake: it's only calm offshore.
Statius is looking for sleep, and the Lord
God is towed beyond this margin's rustlings.
When I was the empress I would canter here,
Slip off my Arab, climb to our tryst,
Happy to play Paris-melted Helen till
The daggers bladed downwards, in between
Collarbone and spine. When the corpse was gone,
His fans unstopped the scents which were his signature

To mark his fall against the steps – this ritual
Led to massacre. Kingcups, marigolds,
Ivy over everything, where Paris strolled
When he was all the rage. Which column
Was it which assigned him to his empress
Who desire slays? – having tasted his desire
During days of arbitrary divorce,
While Uncle Dom went ga-ga over Julia.

I overhear the Britons as they're shown into
Her ruined cave: nymphaeum by the shore
Designed for her by architect Rabirius.
Homage here to Homer as a Paris-trove:
Paris now as Paris, now as Priam old;
As Odysseus, then as Circe, wheedling;
Then a swine, and last Domitian's nothing:
Just a torso tumbled by the water's edge;
No head at all, no neck: an ugly, charred
Crater crudely gouged between the shoulders though.
Yes, Dom did that – and, on a later day,
I squarely sat upon this Lord God's rostrum:
Squares and circles of imperial hue enclosed
In circles, then in lozenges of rosy stone
Bordered by some bilious marble foliage.
The emperor had wanted his divorcee back
After he had forced a death by accident.

A boy is trying on a wig too large for him
As dawn reveals a throne against a crater lip:
Sails of light careen across the bowl below

While the reek of game pervades its wooded slope.
Agonothetes in training jog the lacustrine
Circumference of Diana's glass; a lap or so,
And sweat threads designer stubble as they pass
A poet with his tragedy stitched into him.
Blue is the oval of crater-deep water,
Violets and forget-me-nots. Forget me not.
But Julia, just how was that? A stickler,
Dom was appalled he'd got her up the spout:
Supposed her moral guardian, he ordered her
To down a brew designed to put things right.

Out of all fishermen's hearing, further back
Above the shore, up the overgrown sides of the steep
Enchanted crater rife with beasts below a live
Divinity's retreat – his elevated country seat –
The Lord God's safari park, with ingles there
To clamber up to, laughingly lie down in,
Lovingly to kiss the living, candid skin
Of some delicious shoulder. Ledges a hundred
Feet from where the boys have hung a rope
To swing out from an ilex over water in
The afternoon. Just as I decided to lie down
In the Farnese: jacket spread on small
Square of garden closed by privet hedges:
Prone to sleep while breathing aromatic
Breezes from the oranges; girls abask nearby,
And kids at play, or lost in privet mazes.

Paris, who the gods love, as those about to die:
For there were sea-fights on the lake at times;

Times he crushed me back among bee orchids,
Where he slid inside me, hidden softly then
In fissures which we made our own as spectators lined
A flaming lake – some elephantine ship
Applauded roundly while he soundly rammed me.
Thus the crater rang with clash of arms
As I lay in his arms among the orchids there
Enamoured of my dancer, my divinity.
And then I walked again among the Flavians,
Among their sparse foundations, where an emperor
Transformed into a beetle tried to steer
A passage through a magnitude of ruins
In some humble after, who had hopes perhaps
To be that bumbling hornet next, and irritate
The stroller on his desecrated Palatine
Where Cybele's temple sprouts an ilex patch.

Towed by his slaves beyond sight in the mist,
This is the Lord God seeking the solace of
Utter silence. Julia is dead. Turquoise
In the shallows, as it always was, the lake
Is of the tint her eyes were. Ilexes incline
To dip their leaves, to trail these in the water.
Very dark, they make the turquoise brighter.
Wild barley triumphs over column drums:
Only a toe is left of the emperor's effigy.
Death's angel is God's agent who perniciously
Slew Paris on the steps below the gardens here
As heavy, Hellenistic clouds were gathering.
His terror is the terror of our deviance,
And semen mixed with blood will do it perfectly.

This grubby stone gets booted by the soldiery:
This booted stone was once the head of Paris.
Purple orchids, reddened berries, violets;
Acanthus, ferns and chestnuts, and he came on me,
And then the scent of chestnut blossom smothered us.
And I would twine my snake around a bendy branch
And tell her not to glide into the undergrowth
In case a hawk should stoop – and then I leant
Out and over Rome, against the balustrade
And gazed into the sun as it began to sink
Beyond the Colosseum and the fora there,
Where the balustrade is like an ornate L
Above the Via Sacra and its monuments.

Those daggers bladed downwards as no olive branch
Deflected them: a lovely chestnut struck
By thunderbolt almightiness. The trees
Are full of creepers. In the breeze they trail
Branches to veil the lake's agitation.
Holm oak, and white, white wisteria.
Swans, mallards – most of her nymphaeum
Stopped by stone fall, manna ash and mattresses.
Then I saw *my* dancer on the terrace here,
On the short arm of that L above the Via Sacra.
Sure it was him, well, practically certain:
After all, we'd met before by accident,
Once, outside the Scala, by a traffic-light.

One of my gods for life, but not on high
Except he leapt, this Paris, that Nureyev;
Blossom and the dancer blossom mingled with;

Paris, marble music, perfect star
Shot upwards, elevation as suspense:
My utterly seducer God – my living one
Who never was the Lord God after all;
That Goddish Lord, well, he was merely Dom.
And Rudolf on the terrace, was he worshipping
The Colosseum or the sun? His hands against the stone
Stuck out from a olive track-suit; terrible
How thin he looked. It *couldn't* have been him,
This apparition, knuckles down, palms up:
They were white – as if made of plaster –
Ghosting a dance; the arms not a dancer's.

NOTE: *I was near Rome in April 1991, prospecting in the Alban Hills for a novel about the life and times of Statius. I visited the amphitheatre on the crater which holds Lake Albano (the Mirror of Diana). This amphitheatre is in the grounds of the Villa Barberini – once Domitian's palace, now the Pope's meditative garden. Below it, by the side of the lake, little remains of the nympheum where Domitia conducted her affair with Paris, the greatest mime of his age, later assassinated on the steps leading down from the Farnese Gardens by her imperial husband. Above these steps, a few months before he died, I had, or imagined that I had, my last encounter with Rudolf Nureyev.*

The ancients regarded midday as 'hot and holy', the hour of ghosts. Looking back now at the incident on the balustrade above the gardens, I cannot be sure whether I saw my 'apparition' before or after I went for my siesta among the orange trees. In any case, how could I have been haunted by the ghost of a person who was, at the time, still alive?

Beverley at Iguazú

Her father had diarrhoea:
He didn't care to start
The available trails
In case he got caught short.
The onomatopoeia
Of the falls was lost on him.

Anyway his heart
Was in no condition
To climb the higher trail
Or to get back up
To the Sheraton
From the lower one.

He preferred to stew
On their balcony,
Whiskey in hand,
Feeling he owned
The incredible view
He'd paid to see.

A little train
Had set them down
By the cat-walk
That led to the void.
He hadn't enjoyed
Getting soaked to the skin

As the wide upper river
Flung itself over
The edge into vapour
Brewed in the Devil's Throat:
Garganta del Diablo.
Ok, he said, let's go.

She gloried in the sight,
And in the seeming-slow
Swags of sunlit heaviness
Falling into sheer white
Nothingness whose glow
Suffused her emptiness

And came billowing back
To saturate the spirit
As much as the clothes,
While she stared into it,
Stunned by a chariot
Drawn by a thousand hooves.

He merely found it loud.
She thought it *the* place
To commit suicide.
You'd better wipe your face:
It's ruined your mascara,
Her father replied.

But it was the best brink
She'd ever been brought to,
And while he used the john
In their luxurious room,
She went off alone,
Overwhelmed by its boom;

Astonished that meanderings
Could end in so much turmoil,
Where there were vultures too
Who cleansed their wings
By spiralling towards the clouds
On each humid thermal.

She got invaded by dreams
Of drinking at giant taps,
And following the maps
In the brochures,
Came closer to the vultures
By being ferried across

To a densely jungled bay
In the midst of various chutes.
She met one corpulent lizard
Who scuttled away
To his undergrowth home,
Leaving her to roam,

And later she bathed
In the cool shallows
Of the lower river.
An infinite number
Of curious minnows
Nibbled her throat there.

Under the water,
She loosened her brassiere.
Papa would have frowned:
For what could be crazier
Than this daughter
Of his freeing her breasts,

In order for these
To be eaten by fishes?
They should rid the waterways
Of the little pests.
Ah, but what lovely,
Lovely breasts!

As the Englishman,
Who had danced
A tango with her in
Buenos Aires,
Had called them
When, entranced,

He gently pressed
That part of her
Closer against him,
Moving her with his chest,
Till she seemed to swim
In his element.

The night was terrible.
She found it quite impossible
To sleep or to give vent
To her feelings as
She lay prone
In the bed next to her father's one.

The Sheraton was located
Within the National Park
That closed each evening
At seven o'clock.
The air conditioning
Worked too well:

Its all-devouring roar
Was louder than the falls
That never ceased to spout
And bathed the moon in vapour.
She needed to explore
While no one was about;

But this was strictly
Prohibited by
The authorities,
And anyway
It was dangerous out there,
What with the puma's lair

And that of the jaguar
Somewhere close
In the sub-tropical mass
Of bromeliad and liana,
Densities of grass
And palmetto

Hemmed in by
A precipice
Made treacherous
By numberless cascades
Into canebrakes
Seething with snakes.

Her father kept getting up
And staggering to
The lavatory.
She had to get away
But was clearly in no
Position to do so.

All she could do
Was fret the hours through,
And pace up and down,
Up and down,
On their balcony
Under the moon.

Ode to a Routine

Woken at some ungodly o'clock, you simply
Must get up; though she prefers to do it
Gradually – pushing the alarm to 'doze'
And starting off a drowsy cluck that slowly
Turns into a peck, then unassailable
Crowing minutes after it's been set.
You can't do it like that; have to arise

And go, but though the bulk of you swings clear
Some part remains attached and stretches back
To softness, warmth and slumber under the duvet.
Even so, you manage to pick up
Momentum by attending to essentials:
Teeth may well come first; then the face
Gets splashed, followed by the search for socks.

Each defers unto their own priorities.
Initially we're taught to perform these acts,
Then obliged to repeat them over and over
Till incapable – feels like progress at first.
Later each step's taken in reverse
And represents retreat: while backing out,
We genuflect, like courtiers, to our past.

That's not to say you don't long for the night
Ahead, while loading loathing on the day
Sprung on you too soon, unless brought in
A cup of tea, a juice, a slice of toast;
Or unless, once up and dressed, you make
Yourself a coffee by harsh kitchen light
That only serves to emphasise the dark

Coating the window. Put on your face or your armour
– Shaving for you, for her it's a bra and mascara –
Then run through the checklist: glasses, cap,
Key-chain, money, cards, pass, diary.
What's ahead but the heaviness of what lies
Ahead? The whole day, the whole fucking
Day of it. Hoar frost paints each turf blade

Powder white. You cross the crunchy playing
Field as orange streaks lick the night cowering
Now behind flyovers and factories.
Pressed for time, you'll take the swifter route
Past the stalls in the alley, shutters down,
Though stuff is being unloaded, left and right,
And the costermonger's occupied already;

Getting off with his underage cousin, round
By the back of the bins. The bus arrives,
The one for Seven Sisters. This you board
At the crowded fare-stage opposite Nationwide,
Or, if there's an envelope to post,
The stop up the road, past pre-arranged funerals,
Derelict pleasure-rooms, burnt-out houses of beauty.

Tottenham lurches into the day, and shoals
Of Pakistani school-kids share the aisle
With Roma in Romany dress, Lithuanians,
Workmen with power-drills, priests, mothers up early,
Keen to be first in the queue at the surgery
Or that immigration place. A dark
Smile rolls marbles at some pert remark

On a mobile. High browns hit high fives on blacks.
Hair comes curled in wet-look slicks
Or corn-rowed on cranial plantations.
African London overwhelms these decks:
Suited, or gaudily costumed, redolent
Of cocoa-butter, sandal-wood and musk.
Breathe in as you squeeze past patterned rumps.

Breathe out when alighting next to Tesco's.
Hurried past, the supermarket glows,
Promoting an untimely aura of spruce
Organisation: nearly every till
Attended, all the shelves restocked: the bright
Fluorescents left on every single night
Adding a lustre to the hardening daylight.

Who's a shopper, though, at ten-to-seven?
Bent on earning, curse the lit-up gent
Who stops you while inviting swarms of cars
To hurtle past, until they brake at last
And fingers drum on steering wheels or pick
At noses. Tunes get set and ciggies lit
While time drives on, leaving behind a dam:

Taxis, bikes, commercials and articulated
Tankers; old crocks; luxury jeeps
And other affluent influx from forested Epping;
Alfa Romeos on order to footballers' wives,
And sleek limousines picking up rap artists early
To get to a Nottingham gig – all obliged
To idle as the infantry go by:

Teachers, nurses, plumbers, tea-boys, chefs,
Cleaning ladies, secretaries, clerks,
Management consultants, sales girls, geeks:
Duplicates of those at the other end
Of the city hurrying across the lights:
Their aim's to get wherever you are already.
This is the downside of being in one body

At a single time, though might it not cause
Cancer – being beamed from place to place?
Once upon a time a moving staircase
Proved a source of wonder: rows of lines
Gliding flattened out of metal combs
And turning into steps – the stupid bitch!
Hasn't she learnt to stand on the right? What

Do they teach them, back in Lithuania?
Clutching *The Times* you made a detour for,
Down you thunder, two steps at a time,
Into the intestines of metropolis.
You place yourself exactly on the ledge,
Wary of contact, keeping, as far as you can,
Apart, which could be yards or could be inches.

If you're lucky, something's on its way.
The rails begin to snicker to themselves
About its coming – if you're not, you wait,
Perhaps for aeons. How many deadly hours
Are spent fuming on platforms like ravines
We can't bridge for ourselves? In queues, at counters,
Holding receivers, shifting on our pins,

We fume, until we pass through pearly portals.
Doors arrive and open now. You're off,
Contented, with a seat for once secured;
Although your sedentary movement, well,
It's nothing but another sort of waiting.
Here we go, in our millions, getting where
We want to get to maybe, maybe not.

Packed in together, never deliberately touching,
Nodding to the I-pod, hardly there,
Leafing through the tabloid to some hot spot
Harbouring disaster or desire,
Unless the angle's right to catch a person
Reapplying. As the lips compress,
Daydream on a scheme for her address.

No need to change though. That at least's a relief.
No stampeded steps or gradient passages,
Or girl ahead, who reaches round to tug
Her top down at the back, to read your mind.
This line will take you straight through to Vauxhall,
Passing under roadworks and foundations,
Polishers and hoovers and those nipper things

They use to tidy street and shopping mall.
Purposed or purposeless, you are a merry corpuscle
Jostled in the stream where everything
Is plural – you contribute to the plasma
Circulating through this urban hydra;
Moving along in a grimly juddering silence,
Blasted by a tumult you ignore.

Try to hang on to your inner space, to pray
That you won't get stuck a thousand feet below
Trafalgar Square or Bank or Pimlico.
That's what a person under a train can do.
And they deserve to die in the nastiest way
For the claustrophobic torture of delay
They've wished upon a myriad commuters.

Ground to a halt, in a tunnel, forgotten about.
Certainly no excuse for being impunctual!
Thank God Vauxhall comes sliding into view.
You get off here, to glide up from the bowels,
Oyster an eye and activate the barrier.
Time to buy a roll: its spicy lamb
Gets micro-waved and then you're on your way.

Sneaking past the home of MI6,
Festooned with hearing aids that listen in
To dirty thoughts as well as dirty tricks,
You mount the stairs that lead up to the overland.
A nip here, in the air, unlike the fetid air
You've come from, and a platform crowded
By incoming travellers appropriating marches:

Doing what you're doing in reverse
– Avoiding the *mellée* of Waterloo.
A train drifts in. You choose a window seat,
And now tracks veer away from your trajectory.
Bridges flit by overhead and ads
Unreel along the route and serpentine
Expresses pass with an ephemeral hastiness:

Aimed at the centre, as you travel out,
Passing London's power-station folly,
Streets of roofs, rows of backs, the park;
Town halls, tower-blocks, tops of double-deckers:
Multiples repeated every day;
Multiples compounded by the times
You've seen them pass below these moving panes.

Come rain, come shine, in daylight, in the dark,
At length you reach a duplicate of Clapham
Junction that's a pretty good impression,
Given it's today, of yesterday.
Out you get, descend into a tunnel,
Battle human waves to reach the gate,
Thread the dense arcade and hit the street.

Past Moss Bros, dodge behind a bus to cross
The road and round a corner to your stop.
Now for the worst of all waits, while running short
Of minutes to squander. See how the minutes go down
On a screen inside the shelter outside Debenhams
That once was Alders. Here the juggernaut
Delivering Shoefayre's trainers blocks a lane.

Buses again, pulled up, queuing both ways
To inch past a wing-mirror continentally sized,
Only to get obstructed by some nut
Pulling out from behind the lorry's back.
Stupid bloody bastard! Fucking prick!
These exchanges lead to no reverse:
The jam gets worse, as does the language, but

The passengers can only watch and wait,
Everyone convinced that they'll be late.
Their journey, though, is shorn of any content:
Boredom, rage, revulsion – just a maze
Of vacant forms, and isolated movement
Robbed of all identity by number.
One becomes a cypher, nothing more.

There's no more you. There's one. There's a statistic
Waiting to be counted. That is all.
Eventually one's bus arrives. The driver
Lets the ones on board off first. The ones
Who're waiting then pile in. The doors behave,
And the bus moves at a snail's pace up the rise
Observed by blackbirds perched on someone's grave.

And then, beyond the graveyard and the school,
In an outer borough far removed from one's own,
One's out of the bus and hurrying up a lane,
Then, at a gate-house, proffering an ID,
And the door slides shut behind one. Once inside,
One cuts across a sterile outer yard,
Opens the wicket, closes it of course,

Locks it, proves the lock, and does the same
With the next lock and the next, until one's deep
Inside a place which others can't get out of,
Can't enjoy the freedom one enjoys:
That liberty to travel, to commute
From one place to another, heading back
After one has served one's daily sentence.

Gamma Sango

Splash down, and the wives at Cape Canaveral
Raise their Appletinis to the screen,
Thrilled to glimpse their husbands who have been
A year in space. These brawny cosmonauts

Are being debriefed on some uncharted world:
No fauna, only flora – pteridophytes
Ruled this forest planet. Through their sights
Some ruins were identified – a capital

Overrun by bracken there. The atmosphere
Was kind of dank but breathable, though Don
Began to suffer slightly from what might have been,
Hay fever, and he still does, although Steve

Felt quite ok – but then he's never suffered
That affliction ever. Here's an incident:
Don and Steve are hacking through the fern-
Infested city. Suddenly a kidney-bean-

Shaped pod above them opens with a phlup,
Showering them with its unearthly spores.
Back home, in the suburbs, Steve adores
His crawling baby, picks her up, while Julie

Smiles approval. Then Joanna sneezes.
As he fondly puts her in her cot
Julie notices what looks a lot
Like dandruff on his hair and on his shoulders.

Tutting now, she sweeps the substance off him
Onto the deep pile carpet in the living-room,
Then she drives downtown to meet with Karen.
Sipping soda, Karen's looking glum.

It's Don, you see. It's not that he complains
Since coming back, but all he does is gaze
At television, sneezing. Now it rains.
Steve is driving back from NASA. As he

Skirts the woodland, where their spread begins,
He can't control the Buick – seems as if
His body were immobilised, his hands
Locked to the wheel, and, at a hairpin bend,

He plunges off the road and hits the bank.
Not serious. He's only cracked his head,
And after brief concussion he attempts
To let go of the steering-wheel. He can't.

He's stuck as if with super-glue. The rain
Has stopped now, giving place to fuggy silence.
Steve intensifies his efforts; finally
Succeeds in pulling free – a viscous goo

Loops in sticky strings between the steering-wheel
And him now – an excrescence from his palms.
The stuff disgusts him. With an effort too,
He pulls away from his impacted vehicle

Leaving some damp issue on the driver's seat;
Slowly wipes his fingers on the mossy bank.
Back at home, some ferns are being watered,
While the baby's naked on the carpet,

Sneezing now and then. Steve staggers in:
He's gone a shade of green, but won't explain
What's happened. He just needs to sit and watch
A programme on ecology. It starts to pour

Again now, and the phone rings, and it's Karen
Panicked over Don. So Julie grabs her
Coat and scarf and runs out, telling Steve
To mind Joanna; slips into her beetle,

Backs it from the garage and goes down
The drive, and, at the hairpin, mutters Lord!
Encountering the Buick, but continues
Driving at high speed. Don hasn't stirred

For twenty-four long hours now. A green
Off-putting paste is seeping from the corners
Of his mouth, while on the nearby screen
Some expert is describing the continuing

Destruction of the forests of the Amazon.
Karen's crouching in a corner, shivering.
What's happening? What's happening? She keeps
Asking Julie. Julie reckons they

Should try and lift him out of his armchair
And get him up to bed. Each grabs an arm.
They tug, and tug again, and then his arms
Come off him like discarded husks, and there

Instead are rolled up fern-leaves, closely packed,
But very quickly starting to unfurl
And reach for them. The women both recoil,
And Karen goes to pieces. Don's poor mouth

Lolls wider now, displaying tongues of creeper;
Next his skull splits open: underneath,
Green undergrowth increases as they watch.
Karen, let's get out of here! But she

Will never leave him. Never. Julie snatches
Something near at hand up – it's a flower-pot.
She brings it down on Karen's head, then lifts
Her unresisting body by the arms,

Drags her to the beetle, packs her in
And drives to NASA, where she has a job
Explaining what's going on, first at the barrier,
And later to the sceptical Command.

Karen's gone all stiff now, and it takes
Three tough marines to prise her from the beetle.
Julie heads for home. It hasn't stopped
Raining. Steve has gone all foetal

By the television, and Joanna's still
Uncovered, with her back against the thick
Pile carpet, sneezing. Julie can't believe it.
How can Steve just sit there? He's pathetic,

Leaving her to catch her death like that.
But when she stoops to lift her daughter up,
She finds she can't be budged; a vegetal
Extension like a suction-pad has grown

Out of her diaper, yes, it's eaten through
The carpet and attached itself securely
To the boards. In desperation, gently,
Julie tugs, recalling what occurred

At Karen's house. At length she leaves Joanna
Kicking on the floor and goes for shawls
To cover her. A foul, viridian slime
Seeps slowly out of Steve's unhealthy grin.

It's raining still, if gently, though a downpour
Even so, continuous. The NASA chief
Has gone to visit Don. He tugs the fly-screen
Open, pushes on into the living-room.

Little's left of Don. The place is now
A fernery where kidney-bean-shaped pods
Depend from stag-horns. Foliate rococo
Dominates, and only the tv

Refers to domesticity: it's functioning;
Describing oil disasters. The intrepid
Colonel pushes through the rampant foliage
To switch it off. A loaded spore-pod detonates

Above his head. He brushes off the dust.
Now he's phoning from his jeep to NASA;
Wants the capsule that the men returned in
Checked for any sign of vegetation.

Someone tells him that its doors have jammed,
And men with laser-torches are at go
To burn their way inside it even now.
Sneezing, he insists on safety clothing.

Next he's driving past the buckled Buick
On his way to Steve and Julie's home.
He climbs down to inspect. The fogged interior
Contains a nest of ferns. The windows crack,

As what's within continues to want out.
The capsule cracks at NASA too, before
The insulated guys can use their torches.
Julie teeters from the garage, carrying

A jerry-can as Steve's commanding officer
Rolls up in his jeep. With gritted teeth
She douses home, including Steve and baby,
In petroleum. Joanna's face is

Brilliant green; her body, swathed in shawls,
Is changing shape. Her father's sprouting ferns,
And now a pod hangs down between his knees.
Julie spills out more around the shawls.

The NASA man moves forward to obstruct her.
Kneeling, he attempts to lift Joanna.
Julie sees the dandruff on his shoulders though,
And pours the last all over him. He turns,

His nostrils bleeding green, and grabs her leg.
Ferns unfurl their antlers, and the pod
Cracks between Steve's knees. She wrenches clear,
Scrambles quickly through the ferns and out

Into the kitchen; turns the cooker's gas on.
This lights automatically. She twists
A torch of kitchen-tissue; lights and flings it.
Sheets of flame engulf the fern conservatory.

She dashes to the beetle, as the house
Goes up in smoke behind her: gravel spits
Beneath her tires; but, at the hairpin bend,
The ferns have overwhelmed the Buick and

Thrown up an antlered barrier, expanding
Even as she puts her foot down, crashes
Into it, determined to get through.
Her wheels are caught though. Several pods explode,

And tendrils wind around her spinning axles.
Shucking glass off, Venus flytrap things
Plant suckers on her neck, her breasts, her arms,
Then fasten on her mouth before she screams.

The hairpin bend a few days later. Now
There is no road – no sign of sapient life.
Instead, a forest burgeons in the damp
Stillness broken only by the droplets

Dribbling down the spines of pteridophytes.

The Ogre's Wife

A call for visitors was posted in the church gazette.
Prison seemed my cup of tea. I hunted sinners well
And truly worth it, not the undistinguished sort I'd met

Mired in mere adultery. Did any merit Hell,
As I did, I was pretty sure, for one polluted thought
I'd hesitated to confess? I craved the authentic smell

Of misdemeanour, which is how my pious nature caught
The attention of my Destiny. As I was paying heed
To someone else, one came and sat. The other quickly sought

An exit. Left alone with sin incarnate, I agreed
To struggle for his soul. It felt as if he'd come for me –
A monster others whispered of. His appalling creed

Was soon to give me anxious nights. Because I sensed he saw me
As some catch he'd finish off, that thought of mine took hold:
A prideful notion – that a fiend was destined to adore me,

Making Heaven glad as he was led back to the fold.
Ah, but the assailant proved at least as strong as God!
His gaze was chilling, yes, and yet, it hadn't left me cold,

Although it spoke of irises left bare beneath the sod.
I saw those eyes as you might see them just before you died.
A precipice accompanied the narrow path I trod.

Then a friend went to Japan and sent me a card of a terrified
Woman clamped by her sex to that of a giant octopus:
Pleasured, or disgusted? One was hard put to decide.

At our next encounter, a mistral began to brew in us.
Then he touched – it felt as if my clothing blew away
Together with my sanity. It all seemed too ridiculous

For words. I watched a film that night, about a fish that lay
In wait for males or females, darting out to copulate
Or kill. It was the same with him. I might end up his prey.

I might become his mate. It wasn't clear to him what fate
Was mine. He simply went for me, began to haunt my sleep.
I thought he'd kill me. Wanted out. But it was now too late,

And I deserved to be destroyed, for coveting this deep
Liaison with a source of darkness. Then they let him out.
He'd got my number off me while I'd still had hopes I'd reap

The benefits of winning him for Jesus. More devout
Than sensible, I'd prayed to save his soul as if my life
Depended on it. Did such ardour put my faith in doubt

And our Redeemer test it then by making me the wife?
If so, He handed me the role I'd dreamt of in a drama
Set on earth to mirror Hell. That gaze cut like a knife

On meeting in a bleak cafe – little of the charmer
About this one. I was disembowelled there and then. The joy
Would come, I knew, when every last impediment of armour

Fell away, and, naked, I was his: a chattel to employ
Exactly as he willed. So be it. Here stood his lamb for the slaughter.
But I was too eager. I bore him first a girl and then a boy.

Hostages? Accomplices. He needed son and daughter,
Never threatened. Still, I felt it foolish to oppose him.
He might then reject the bed, forsake the conjugal quarter

Of his life, its one consoling refuge. So to swim
Against his current wasn't right. Nirvana, if release
From pent-up urgency, gets enhanced by fear, however slim

The chances are that you can circumvent the need for peace
That moves your executioner. After we'd had intercourse,
I'd lie there, panic on the ebb – would contact the police,

If I could get away, that is. I never did, of course;
Hugely humbled, grateful that he'd chosen not to stop
My breath on this occasion. Church would never bless divorce

From duty allotted, namely to stay the devastating crop
Of murders if I could. Although I failed, and failed again,
My forgiveness mattered. He was just the one on top

Of the situation, just as the will of powerful men
Crucified our Saviour. Me, I lay in ecstasy
Beneath him. Psychiatrists may learnedly insist that when

I went with him initially some suicidal part of me
Came to the fore – acknowledged – though I did not wish for death
As such. To risk it as I rose to pleasure: agony

Perfected – as it might please Mary, when she received that shibboleth,
For the angel to appear in his inordinate splendour,
Glory ablaze, to experience the empyrean breath

And be consumed by Word made Fire from which no shield could
                                                    defend her
Any more than my presence could protect the girls he came
Across on his hunting trips, my hubby, for whom there was no surrender

That was acceptable, other than mine, no offering the shame
Of meek desire as your Pekinese will, set on by a mastiff,
Nor need anyone declare that I should bear much blame.

I was a decent girl, after all, albeit rather passive
While at the convent where you were either principled or damned.
Some of the girls there opted for damnation in that oppressive

Atmosphere at variance with the times. Having had it rammed
Into them that sex was wrong, they took a flippant view
Of immaculate conception, and were sure the sisters shammed

Their abstinence. They masturbated, everybody knew!
Wine was good for nothing else but to get pissed, party and shag on.
Not in the least like them, I really thought that it was true

That sex was wrong. I was not prepared to jump aboard the wagon
Of their promiscuity. Lust was a covert activity
Hardly even sanctified by marriage – devised by a dragon

Or worse. How could you accommodate both piety
And arousal, or justify an appetite for the soiled
Hungers of the lower body? Cleanliness and Chastity,

These were the Cardinal Virtues, whereas having sex embroiled
You in a cauldron no one ever clambered from unscathed –
To perish in the bestial act, though, left the soul unsoiled,

By way of being a sort of retribution – you were saved,
Or at least your soul was. So, for me, to hazard being deprived
Of life made sex conceivable. I had this engraved

As well: my risking death in wedlock actually revived
My partner's chances of remission. Thus did the Lord ordain
That I should serve. The sinner might be saved if I survived.

None of his crimes weighed much compared to what God stood to gain
Through me. Victory over Satan would be absolute
When at last we brought this being, penitent, to cleanse the stain

On his conscience. When he went hunting, I would choose the route,
Sat in the van beside him. He would roll his window down
Since he declared that he could scent the ripe yet unplucked fruit

As if he were a unicorn. He joked about the renown
Of this beast, and how it pierced the zone that it identified
Even as it sought the unsullied lap, but then he'd frown,

For he wasn't always correct, nor did he ever once decide
To abandon his plan if the girl had been with a beau or had a bun
In her oven. He acted on impulse, just like the fish, however he tried

To justify his choices. Certainly the Infernal One
Prompted him as much as I was moved by the Righteous Being.
Then it was *my* job to lower a window, always with our son

Or daughter sitting on my knee, clearly installed for the seeing,
Offer the lift from which the girl at the verge would never alight.
Into the back of the van she'd climb – and there was no fleeing

For her after that from what was an inevitable fight
Between good and evil, between my spirit and his: a desperate
Engagement this, rendering her contribution trite.

He took her home occasionally, and I must needs commiserate
With the creature, 'Make your peace, my dear. The chosen are but few.'
I meant it: these were the ones he chose to rape and lacerate

At leisure. Others, alas, he took by force without ado
Then strangled on the floor of what he called his chariot
Of desire. I used to watch in the mirror. The view

Gave me a way to assess her worth. Did she tarry at
The stake, or did she embrace it greedily? And did she
Seek my glance in the glass? Oh, I was worse than Iscariot,

In her estimation, I guessed; but if she succumbed too easily
Then I'd report to our Lord that she was not for Paradise.
Purgatory for her then, at the very least. For me,

Whatever her response, once he'd gone inside her thighs
She deserved the rest – intact no longer, had she ever been –
Just a slut who humped with him before my very eyes.

Why did I let it happen, though? I still relive each scene,
Reflecting on my inertia, as I watched in that mirror, appalled.
Perhaps because normality would right itself between

One killing and the next. We lived at peace. And if I'm called
Abettor, then I claim this mitigating victory:
When it happened, Love prevailed, and Lucifer was mauled.

My husband dug their graves beforehand on our property.
He tipped them in, he covered them, stamped the turf down tight,
Then, to receive my blessing, afterwards he'd come to me.

Yes, and I knew everything, yet still survived the night.
This was a miracle. Was he not Mortality made flesh?
And since God died as Jesus, he'd killed God, he'd killed the light!

Ah, but in the double bed, where, bloodied, we'd enmesh,
I was Death's entire salvation, by God's Grace appointed
Gleaner of this abject portion else left behind in the thresh

Of spirits winnowed at the Trumpet, when the world's anointed
Rise on the Day of Judgement, making all creation whole.
. . . Yesterday, though, an inspector called and it was pointed

Out to me that certain secrets land you up in gaol.
Recently too I have gathered that the wife of a neighbouring ogre
Just got thirty years for not being able to control

His appetite. My outlook's altered, since I took up yoga.

Silent Highway

1. *Heraclitus*

Apotheosis! Arsenals of the sky
Ablaze, exploding, crimsoning the crowns
Of storm clouds over Woolwich with its furnaces
Producing the great barrels of our guns.
Apotheosis, mist-suffused at sunrise
As the duck wing over Dagenham Breach.
Those decent acres have been overwhelmed
By the sky's double, Father Thames,
The Tiber's brother, leaning on his couch
Of bales and bundles, ever outward bound;
His oar is more a cricket-bat, his ewer
Overflows with tributes such as Isis
Brings to bless his bridges and his Pool.
Her masons swear by Cleopatra's needle.
There she dances with her timbrelled maids –
As high on chants as any Hari Krishna.

Apotheosis, Phoebus in his car,
Driving away demonic clouds with deafening
Percussion in the vanguard of their flashes,
Just like Alice scattering the cards
To call a halt to rolling heads,
While William and Mary ascending
Get as far as that wide ceiling there
In the painted Hall of Greenwich where

We chorus, Tyranny avaunt!
Avaunt, ye darksome powers, most inglorious!
Unconstitutional monarchies, rights divine!
Now let's be enlightened, leave a space
Between the buildings for the Queen
To get a view of Canary Wharf,
Sir Christopher, no wider than her house is.

*   *   *

Heraclitus knew about rivers,
Knew that in differing, banks agree,
Talked of a backward-turning connection,
Like that of a bow or a lyre.
You could say the path of a river
Is both straight and crooked at once,
Since the water flows in one direction
While each bend conducts it in another.
Thus it is the Thames wends north at Westminster,
Thus it is it swings due east at Southwark:
Impulses reversed though, as the tide comes in.
The path either way is one and the same,
For we are all flowing through time.
The river is day and night, winter and summer,
War, peace, youth and old age.
It quenches the sun, and it sets the moon
Ablaze with its rippling dance.
Into the selfsame river
No one can ever step twice,
For dropsical Heraclitus knew
That the universe flows like a river

And that the river is fire.
Think of the Great Fire of London
Sweeping across old London Bridge,
Heating the starlings, the cut-waters,
Warming the current, or think of Rum Quay
On fire in the blitz: a river of flame.
A river is like a book, you can get lost
In it – as it was said of the book
Of Heraclitus, it would take a Delian
Not to drown in it.

*   *   *

The Thames is rising fast
While you play me without haste
At a game I'm meant to lose,
Though you end up in my shoes
And tell me we might stay
Together, were we free.

And why should you be lying?
You move beneath me sighing
At the high tide of our dream,
While the river flows upstream
To flood the reach profusely
As you spread about me loosely.

But how we are just now
We both of us well know
Isn't easily surpassed
So it better be the last,

For love will surely start
To tear our lives apart.

Then everyone around us
Will hate us and confound us,
For it's only at the neaps
One wades across these deeps;
And now if we go further
We will drown in each other.

2. *Pocahontas*

Thus the river sanctions love and lust
For water, being water, isn't dust;
And sailors like their ladies in less clothes
Than might seem proper – light shifts and bare toes.
Call it, then, a short chemise, or mini-skirt,
That Nannie wears on board the Cutty Sark.
Weird perhaps for a clipper ship
To be christened after a sister of Old Nick:
'But Nannie, far above the rest
Hard upon noble Maggie prest
Whose spring brought off her master hale
But left behind her ain grey tail,
And when to drink you are inclined
Or Cutty-sarks run in your mind,
Think, ye may buy the joys o'er dear,
Remember Tam O'Shanter's mare'
And Nannie's speed, which brought the tea

From China each new season with a tail
Of old rope painted grey within her clutch
When she sailed in past Greenwich with
A stack of well-aired Twankey in her hold.
Think of this silent highway – in its heyday
Anything but silent – silent now;
But not when Pocahontas sailed this way,
On a sparkling morning – cloudless blue,
A light wind helping and a silvery haze
Improving London town. But it was hard
To walk so, in moccasins on cobble-stones:
Hard to be ignored by James the First,
Though he looked fine in the palest blue
On a foaming, fiery horse, and then,
After a nicer interview with dour
Sir Walter Raleigh, feverish, in the tower,
Who knew the doings of the Powhatan,
Hard to die at Gravesend, of consumption,
Within a year, her long anticipation
Heralding so short a stay in London.

*   *   *

Some have come in dread, Sir Henry Morgan
        being but one example, clapped in irons,
Damned to hell, a braggart buccaneer
        heading for the dock and execution,
Only to be dubbed a knight and sent
        back to Jamaica, governor of the island . . .

Some have started out from here, aboard
    the vessels built at William Fairbairn's works
At Millwall, in the engineering shops,
    at the joiners, on the pattern-makers' benches,
In the foundries, in the smithies;
    in the yards with every stout appurtenance
For constructing ocean-going tonnage.
    Here were built the *Grappler* and
The *Megaera* for the navy, and
    'the largest vessel floated', the *Great Eastern*.

Iron-hulled, the *Eastern* was intended
    to unnerve the sirens of the Cape.
Her length was more than three times that
    of the Monument on Fish Street
While her breadth was equal to Pall Mall's.
    Promenades around her deck
Afforded a walk of a quarter-mile.
    Designed by Isambard Kingdom Brunel,
She boasted a brace of engines, two propellers,
    and her bridge's 'cellular' construction.
She *combined* the might of steam
    by using paddle-wheels *and* screws,
Featured ten boilers, five funnels
    and a hundred furnaces – or more.
Her paddle-wheels were sixty feet in height;
    each one of them some ninety tons in weight.

'A Floating City,' so averred Jules Verne:
    and one required to lay the Atlantic cable.

She alone could store its miles of wire.
    and when she afterwards became
A transatlantic liner, her interior
    was fitted out at horrible expenditure.
The ladies saloon and the grand saloon
    were ornaments with lustres,
Lamps and rosy, risqué pictures.
    Skylights lit the dance-floors. Gilded pillars
Framed the stairs whose genuine mahogany
    led baluster by baluster towards the upper deck.
Prospective passengers though took fright
    at the sight of this female Colossus
And so she never prospered, the *Great Eastern*,
    failing at times to answer to her helm,

Maybe her myth would have been the more glorious
    had she gone down, bullies,
Had she gone down.
    But ignominiously, she ended up
Conveying coals from Newcastle to London,
    then was sold for scrap.

       *   *   *

'A well-featured but wanton young girl'
Playing in her pre-nubile nakedness
Within the Jamestown settlement:
Leapfrogging, turning cartwheels with the cabin-boys,
Powhatan, her father, chief of chiefs,
A tall and well-proportioned man
With a sour look, his head inclined to grey,

His beard so thin it seems no beard at all.
His warriors, six foot tall, are clad in pelts
Which barely hide their privities;
Live garter-snakes, their ornaments,
The right side of the scalp shaved with a shell,
The left side worn like a knotted tail.
They paint their faces blue or white,
And put on buckskin leggings in the fall.
Their priest totes a snake-skin head-dress
Stuffed with moss, and at their ceremonials,
They dine on tasty maize-cakes, broiled
Fish on hurdles, guinea fowl and venison,
With fresh oysters, baked inside their shells,
As for their entertainment are dismembered
The bodies of their captives piece by piece
While they yet live. The cultivated gentlemen
Of Jamestown, on the other hand
Look especially grand in their Sunday
Satin or taffeta finished with slashes.
They cultivate rich pinking and embroidery
And doff their plumes at the Eucharist
Before they hang the colonist who has missed
The service for three Sundays in succession.

'Bid Pocahontas bring hither
Two little baskets
and I will give her white beads
To make her a chain.'

3. *Windrush*

Into what world, then, came such noble savages,
Or the Huguenots, or the refugees, or the immigrants?
They slid beneath the city, shot the bridge,
A risky business in the time of Pepys.

Then London Bridge was crammed with leaning houses,
Chimneys, water-mills and traitors' heads,
And London's river seemed indeed a pool.
And if they trudged up Watling Street from Dover

Gog and Magog stood guard on London's gate:
The sole survivors of some monstrous brood,
Offspring of the thirty-three hard daughters
Of the Emperor Diocletian. They had murdered

All their husbands; then, being set adrift,
Reached Albion, and there fell in with demons.
Out of their union sprang a race of giants
Seventeen foot high, a plague of freaks

Extirpated by the resourceful Brut.
He only spared Magog and Gog, their leaders.
Led in chains to London, these were taught
To serve as porters at the palace, now

The Guildhall, where their golden-armoured effigies
Have stood at least since the reign of Henry V.
Their oldest figures went up in the blaze
That swept the bridge and burnt out London's plague.

The next ones came down with the blitz, but still
They stand in their most recent incarnation,
Only nine foot high, but looking Roman,
Now *inside* the hall. With civic pride,

They flank musicians in the wooden gallery.
And if you climb the spiral stairs within
Wren's monument, constructed with the cash
Meant for the Great Fire's orphans, for a view

Of Tower Bridge where the warship lies at anchor,
Or look out west towards Saint Paul's or north
Across the city's gleaming glass cathedrals,
Or glance below, at taxis in a jam,

And pleasure boats and launches, tugs and barges
Glimpsed between tall spires, mediaeval buttresses,
Satellite dishes, ventilation apertures,
Then you will sense that Gog and his companion

Still serve London, working now as cranes,
By swinging round prefabricated slabs
Or dropping chains to be attached to canisters
Amid the whine of saws, the clang of metal.

*   *   *

'Sweet Thames, run softly, till me end I song,
Me quit the West Indies and the journey be long.

I daddy fly a spitfire. He never come back.
I ma, she teach the school, but we living in a shack.

When Mr Clement Atlee be driven by his wife
In a Hillman Minx, we think, this is the life!

When Mr Harold Wilson make a bonfire of Controls
We come to Great Britain to repair their holes.

And when me see the chimneys ranged along the shore
Me say with all them factories no one can be poor.

Though me shiver for I life on the Tilbury Docks
Me think about the lucre me be putting in a box.

But they say, if we admit them dammit that'll mean
An ever greater influx of Jamaicans on the scene.

So they grudge we our jobs and they don't let we places,
Because we ain't them – and we don't wear *they* faces.

Thing is that they can't make head or tail of how we talk.
Thing is that they don't say good day to we at work.

And if we ride the bus then no one sit beside we,
And they all hide their eye and they rail and they deride we,

And we sleeping in the street, and it hard for we to stick it,
But then me think at least we can beat them at the wicket.

All the sweat of working be to set things up back home,
But it's more than fifty year, and me still on the roam.

Man, it's just the women here who make we feel alive:
Had I share of them since the day me arrive.

Ain't they lain beside we, the smooth night long?
Sweet Thames, run softly, till me end I song.'

          *   *   *

The canine dead wash up on the Isle of Dogs.
    But under that sheer obelisk of glass there
The docks are like capital letters made of water.
    Water and glass... Madonna's penthouse, Bowie's...

But 'back in the 1840's most of London's
    water still came from the Thames,
Polluted by outfall from sewers,
    by stable dung, putrefied sprats and guano,

And by the rubbish and offal thrown into it
    from slaughter-houses, knackers' yards,
Tanneries and tar works. The colour
    was a greeny black, and its consistency so thick

That each time the tide went down
    a greasy, foul-smelling scum was deposited over the mud.
In 1849 the drainage system –
    if so noisome a collection of leaking pipes,

Uncovered cess-pits, stinking gullies,
    rotting privies and gas-filled sewers
Could be called a system at all
    combined with the shallow, overcrowded

Burial grounds and a pall
    of smoke-filled, disease-ridden fog
To produce a cholera which could kill
    four hundred people a day.'

I doubt that this affected the robust
    river pirates, or the night plunderers, or the light horsemen
Or the heavy horsemen who relieved
    the overladen game ships of their strap,

And generally went furnished with habiliments
    designed to hide all manner of commodities:
Sugar, coffee, cocoa and pimento,
    carried on shore by means of an under waistcoat

Harbouring pockets all round, and also
    surreptitious bags, pouches, socks
Tied to their midriffs underneath their trowsers.
    They pilfered there in consort with the game

Watermen whose habit was to place
    the oil-casks upside down in their lighters,
So that the oil could seep out
    and into the false bottoms of their craft.

Then there were the scuffle hunters, good
    at taking advantage of spills and disputes.
Meanwhile, on the water side by Blackfriars,
    clusters of mudlarks might be seen

At work where the barges were lying.
    They would prowl about at low water
Pretending to grub for old nanny tails, iron:
    boys and girls mostly, from eight to fourteen,

Ragged, in a very filthy state.
    Sometimes they would get between the barges,
And one of them would lift the other up
    to toss the coal-lumps out into the mud,

Coal they would pick up afterwards,
    and sell among the lowest class of people.
And some were old women who would wade
    in the grey mud up to their knees.

One of these might be seen at Wapping,
    her bonnet tied with a handkerchief,
Picking up coals from the river's bed
    and putting them into a bag she had:

Coals she would offer for sale in the town,
    wandering barefoot in an old gown,
        her coal-bag balanced on her head.

        *   *   *

4. *Uncle Rufus*

Launched with a huge array of cast-iron ornament,
Notably shields displaying the crest
Of the London, Chatham and Dover Railway Company,
Daubed in heraldic colours but declared
By the public a monstrosity, Blackfriars
Merged with the nearby bridge of Saint Paul's.
The merger brought it pulpits and parapets.
Then on the 15th of June, 1982, four years after
The assassination of a rather decent pope,
The body of Roberto Calvi was found at the end of a rope
Beneath the granite arches of this bridge;
His hands tied behind his back,
His jacket pocket weighed down by a brick.

Blackfriars marks a corner of that square
Mile that keeps the city split off from the town.
Deeply involved in a fraudulent Vatican loan
Which led to the implosion of his banco,
Calvi fled to England carrying a portmanteau
Filled with ambrosial banknotes. Banking on a deal
With Opus Dei, whereby they would acquire a
Holding in his bank by paying off the Mafia,
Calvi was obliged to bankroll Propaganda Due.
Bankrupt – and corrupted by its puppet-master, Gelli –
While frantically attempting to plug the gaping hole
In his bankbooks, he had agreed to launder
The drug engendered profits of the Corleone family.

He never laundered the money though. Instead,
He 'borrowed' it to keep his ship afloat.
Opus Dei reasoned that with Calvi dead,
The total collapse of his stocks would result
And this in turn dislodge their powerful
Enemies in the Curia, opening the way for them
To gain total dominance of the Vatican.
It was revealed by a Mafia informer
That Calvi had been strangled by the Mafia's
London based heroin traffic manager.
Bridges are the sacred responsibility
Of the Whitefriars of Paris. But this is the bridge
Of the masons, of the shadowy

Practitioners of corporate piracy, the mighty
Of the mercantile world; those who dictate
That Canary Wharf shall be shaped
Like an obelisk and that its shadow
Shall fall over Hawksmoor's church
With the pyramid beside the gate at Limehouse.
Some say Captain Smith was a mason,
And so was Powhatan, who knew him
By some sign – and this saved Smith,
And it was nothing to do with Pocahontas!
In this reach, on an August night in 1989,
Two hundred young people were partying
Aboard that tidy pleasure boat, the *Marchioness*...

*   *   *

A summer-barge of jollity
Afloat on bags of lolly,
Members of the quality
Took coffee on 'The Folly'.

There the wits would gad about
And squawk like pretty Polly.
Nothing to be sad about
When frequenting 'The Folly'.

The lounge of every wealthy earl
With nothing in his nolly,
As well as Addison and Steele.
How splendid was 'The Folly'.

But where Queen Mary once had trod
Came trollop veiled in trolly,
Many a gambler's curse on God
Was heard aboard 'The Folly'.

Then drapers' smudged apprentices
With city girls most jolly,
After shop was shut and all,
Would sail up to 'The Folly'.

At length the boat grew scandalous
And Amsterdam's plump Molly
Proved the poor man's Tantalus
Below decks, on 'The Folly'.

At last it fell into decay
Abandoned by each dolly.
Sold for firewood, so they say,
The Somerset's old 'Folly'.

*   *   *

Three hundred miles of embankment between
Westminster Bridge and the Nore;
All much improved by the Romans
Who could handle the spade or the spear:
Navvies just as much as soldiers,
Paviors of the world beneath their feet,
Bridge-builders, ferrymen, waders of fords.

Downstream, where the river widens,
Eager to engage the seas it bullied in imperial times –
When 'all the liquid world was one extended Thames' –
Monks laid claim to marshland, making fields,
Though Dagenham's fields were overrun
By floods no river wall could quite accommodate;
Old as the turns of its stream, though it be,

With its moorlog of buried yew tree,
Antler, hazel, brushwood, fir . . .
The stone embankments put in place by Bazalgette
Annoy my uncle, Rufus Noel-Buxton.
He placed the river in chains! he maintains,
Quoting some inscription to the architect.
Uncle Rufus waded the Thames

At Westminster, to prove the Romans did it.
Do you like wading in dark water?
May I invite you to the old Westminster Ford? –
Not just any old ford but the most famous ford in the land.
It took you across the largest river in England.
A ford famous before the Romans
But paved by them along with Watling Street.

Watling Street, the road from the Cinque Ports
To Chester in the far north-west of England,
Tackling the sluggish Thames at Westminster
Just at the point where it was very broad
And pitched against its own intended flow –
'Slowed' by the swings of the river
At Charing Cross and at Pimlico.

Well, do you want to do it? Do you like dark water?
Soaked through, in his galoshes, he spooks
The Upper House, rousing Lords from slumber:
'I only swam two strokes!'
A Labour peer, hereditary, unhappy
That his claim was neither based on merit
Nor on more than a single generation,

Uncle Rufus championed emigration
More or less for everyone except
For ancient Britons, if they could be found,
For bird-watchers, for birds, for water-violets…
He liked to talk to herons, being tall,
And waded here, and further up, at Brentford
Composing poems as he strode or strove

To stride across each waterway, imagining
Himself a Roman soldier known as Flavius
And getting published by a little Press,
His poem sanctioned by the Poet Laureate
And someone who didn't know much about gods;
But thought that the river was a strong brown god –
Sullen, untamed and intractable...

Envoy

For bird-watchers, for birds, for water violets,
You need to get up further, though at Battersea
A cormorant has settled near the house-boats,
Ducks come dabbling by the shore and gulls
Mew back at the squeals of brakes on the bridge.
In autumn swifts will fling themselves skywards
Above the Port authority's 'Driftwood' –
A barge employed for mooring other barges
Laden with containers. Past it flow
The sodden newspapers, the spars
Of ancient brooms, the toilet-seats and cans
We have come to expect now of our careless age.
The water is diagonally divided by
The jumbos floating down towards Heathrow.
It's best we leave the river though at Westminster,
For this is where it's at its most rhetorical,
A reliable surge past an insecure seat of government,
Ever on time with its tides, unhurried...
Imagine it as it might have been a century ago,
Just as Monet painted it, envisaging
His indigo impression, twists of cloud,
The water like a nocturne by Debussy,
And flecks of gold transforming tall Big Ben
Into a tower as enchanted as Rapunzel's...

My Part in the Downfall of Everything

A Satire on Deceit

My part in the downfall of everything
Kicks off with my genes. Who knows what
They may have been a party to
That brought about the inexorable loss
Of some original state harmonising

With the earth, with beasts and birds
And blooms in the Nativity of Time?
Expulsion from this previously integrated realm
Must have seemed complete by 1933
For any cavalry officer who had seen

Service in the Kaiser's army
Fifteen years before, but who now
Found himself held back at the Ministry
Next to a gutted *Reichstag*. Here,
For the lack of authoritative stamp,

My Jewish '*Opa*' cooled his heels
In an anteroom as General Goering addressed
The rest of a Zionist delegation.
Brandishing a wad of clippings, Goering
Launched into a harsh denunciation

Of those among the populace responsible
For spreading anti-Nazi propaganda
In Britain and America – gross exaggerations,
Detailing atrocities that constituted
Fabrications. 'Put a stop to these

Libellously false reports immediately
Or I shall not be able (or inclined)
To guarantee the safety of the Jews.'
One among the summoned pointed out
That bits of what the papers said were true,

Friends had been subjected to attacks,
Others murdered. 'Use a plane
And shavings fall,' said Goering.
After that, my grandfather was sent,
At the Reich's insistence, to London;

Charged with the task of calming down
The press, but with an urgent mission
Of his own, which was to caution those at the helm,
Non-Jewish leaders and prominent peers,
That the fascist flood would overwhelm

European Jewry pretty soon.
Emigration was the only way
To counter this, with the National Home
In Palestine the appropriate place
Of refuge. At a later meeting

Back in Berlin, one *Hauptmann* Von Buelow
Quizzed him: Did he not agree
That Zion and Valhalla
Happened ideologically
To be pretty closely related?

This was a kinship to be exploited.
Mastery and destiny might grow
Sturdy in stature, if in separate lands.
Send us off, please, begged the eager Zionists.
The Reich was half-inclined to let them go.

Later on, my uncle and my father,
Lederhosened lads then, in Berlin,
Blond and blue-eyed, both of them,
Were stopped by other boys and urged
To join the Hitler Youth. This taken in,

Our family got out. Their flight
Was booked that very day. Let us however
Return to the *Hauptmann's* insight:
Hebrew and Viking both seem 'preferred',
Both vouchsafed a secure abode;

Being 'chosen', more than merely good,
Vindicated, even 'Antinomian'; each with a hand
On the plane that bears down on the wood
So that shavings fall. Justified in
Choosing to protect the useful criminal,

After the war, for instance;
Recognising power's 'aura', blest indeed!
With Grace a state – of being – not
An aspiration or to be attained,
But yours in essence, birthright of your race.

Clearly this was the mindset governing the
Project for the New American Century,
Seeded as it was with dual citizens:
US Israelis, taking their cue
From the Stern Gang, steeped in atrocity:

Murderers loathed by the Major my father
Became. No Zionist he, but emphatically
A Briton now, although a refugee;
Roundly condemning that terrorist cell,
Because they destroyed the King David Hotel

With fellow Brits in it during the Mandate.
The killers were the fruit of genocide;
Orphans of the killed, who mocked that passive
Herding to the gas that characterised
The 'cattle' of the Holocaust.

In them a fiercer wish, a more aggressive strain,
A *sabra* spirit ripened, armed with spikes.
The prickly pear epitomised *these* kikes.
More at one with the sword than with the slain.
So chosen chose the chosen, wiping history

Clean of past aggression, retribution, guilt,
While bound as in a tryst to some new Axis.
Armed to the hilt though in their sense of right,
Choosing to lead, choosing America also;
Deeming US leadership to be

'Good for America and for the world.'
To think of oneself, therefore, as a mine
Armed with pins intended to destroy
The sadly inept, almost rudderless
Progress of that leaking barque *Democracy*.

Dark union of Mossad, the CIA
And assorted skulls and bones, with their techniques
For washing brains, their operatives
Automatised – in order to be dropped
Into the field of ever blacker ops.

Ops that see destruction as regenerative;
A view espoused by the Pope in Sade's *Justine*,
Ops that are cloaked in deceit. Take Nero's Rome
In ashes, and the Christians who became
His torches – blamed for setting all aflame.

Take Luther's friend, then enemy, Agricola,
Who preached that faith alone permitted Grace,
That such a state enabled one 'to grow
Guiltless forever, like a tree
That buds and blooms, nor seeks to know

The law by which it prospers so . . .'
Agricola rejected the commandments,
For souls should relate to the Gospels alone,
There being no Old Testament in Christ;
A view that appeals to the powerful now.

All that's asked for is to be devout.
Prosper then, press forward with the plane
And let the shavings fall as bodies fall
From blazing towers. And blame it, blame it all
On those you use for torches.

Be devout though solely in your aim.
You have a goal. Pursue it. Serve your god.
But after all, your god is Mammon.
He is arse and arsenal. Isn't his purse
As vast as the pit is bottomless?

Doesn't he deem his war-chest more than vast
In respect of what's needed to blast
Everything in the Middle East
To smithereens? Thusly to increase his grip
On time which is what money is,

He can bribe Nayirah as a witness
So that she may testify before a wide-eyed Congress
That she has seen Kuwaiti babies
Taken out of incubators, causing them to die.
Daughter of the ambassador to the USA,

Didn't she get a penthouse off of Daddy
For blurting out that lie which galvanised
The rest of us with this concocted crime?
Sheik and rabbi, president and priest,
All go along with the protocols of the Elders.

Time is oil. Power is time,
And money worships profit.
So if a war is what you seek to profit by,
Make it happen, let your fleet be bombed
By 'Kamikaze' pilots, human drones.

You are immortal, you are the old man,
The one in the mountains, old, but showing none
Of the signs of age, directing your assassins
So that they penetrate deeply, deeply
Into the encampment of your enemy –

Or was the myth a slander from the start?
Those suicidal pot-heads from the mountains,
In the main, Crusader fabrications:
The murder of King Conrad of Jerusalem
More than likely set up by the Lionheart.

This is not to say that such sheer perfidy
Is characteristic only of the West;
Those engaging in another's game
Play by their opponent's rules.
Apartment blocks blow up, get flagged

As Chechen fouls – when wired by
A covert State administry. Today
All deal in falsity, taking on the uniform
Of the foe, doctoring the evidence.
The truth being simply what one cannot know.

Blow up your own citadel to justify
The ransack of another sovereign land.
Gag protest – in the name of (your) democracy.
Try on the jackboot, even as you preach
'Lead us not into dictatorship.'

My part in the downfall of everything
Includes my inability to do anything
About all this, though I live beneath the cloud
Of a Cabal, though the times are rotten
And the secular fail, I do nothing,

Coping merely with my own conspiracies,
Petty sins, white lies, but little more.
My father fought and died. Our generation
Ambles through an age of drab permissiveness,
Insulated from each distant war

Waged on others by the very affluence
Milked from these stings and their violence;
Careless of how loathed we are
For siding with some nest of wasps
While we try on garments in the mall.

It's evident, though, that your
Enemy's enemy can become your pal.
And thus it is that *Eretz Israel*
Reinforces Isis via the choppers of the Yanks,
And this is all down to think-tanks

Such as the PNAC. It sure smells
Like a coup to me and to Wesley Clark
And Cynthia McKinney. Voice after voice
Gets raised now, that of Barbara Honegger,
Susan Lindauer's also, calling for an end to it,

An end to the deceit. That wily knight
Bertrand de Born – wasn't he
Surrounded? Wouldn't he keep
His foes at bay by setting these against
Themselves, each at a neighbour's throat?

It's past belief, the sins religions mask;
The earth a promised land until we trashed the place;
Restoring it, our Herculean task.
Understand that others stoke divisiveness,
And harems aren't laid on for one in Paradise.

The Delegation

Excommunicate, his people cowering under papal interdict,
Him unwilling to accept, as arch-bishop, Cardinal Stephen
Langton, Innocent's thunder-tongued favourite, champion
Of Thomas à Becket, his father's own 'troublesome priest',

Beziers fallen, to crusade against the wayward troubadours of Oc,
Children marching in ecstatic pelt to shipwreck or to slavery,
And it being easier to extract a Hebrew's teeth than ever to get
At his cash, with Langton and the barons plotting mutiny,

John Lackland sent off messengers in secret, namely, Thomas
Hardington, with one Ralph Fitz-Nicholas, and a clerk called Robert
London – charged to seek Murmelius, Morocco's mighty son;
Lord of Africa and Spain, also known as Miramumelinus.

When these three emissaries arrived at the court of this prince,
They found at the first gate Saracen knights keeping guard,
Each with naked blade. And at the second gate, that of the palace
Itself, they endured a frisking from a larger paynim horde,

Armed to the teeth, attired now more handsomely, fiercer
And more noble than the first; and each enforced security
With scimitar in hand: then, at the door to the innermost chamber,
There was a still greater number, finer, stronger, fiercer than before.

Having though been peaceably conducted in by leave of the Emir,
These envoys, on behalf of their distant master, England's King,
Saluted with due reverence that monarch who consented to receive them.
Earnestly they stammered out the reason for their daring to approach,

At the same time handing him a sealed letter, which an interpreter,
Summoned by his master, then construed. The gist of it was this:
Their king would voluntarily give up to him himself and his kingdom,
And if he pleased would hold the realm as tributary unto him.

Abandoning the Christian faith, which he considered false,
John would adhere to the law of the prophet Mahomet.
When he grasped its purport, the Emir – who was of middle height,
Of manly deportment, eloquent and circumspect –

Closed the volume that he had been looking at – a sovereign
Given to study, it seemed, seated at his desk. At length,
After deliberating as it were for a time with himself, he replied:
'I was just now looking at the book of a wise Jew and a Christian

Named Paul, which is written in Greek, and his deeds and his words
I am taken by. One thing however concerning him displeases me.
And that is, that he failed to stand firm to the faith in which he was born,
But turned, turned to another – a deserter and a waverer –

And I say this with regard to the King of the English, your lord,
Who forsakes his saviour's pious and most pure creed,
Under which he was born, and desires, flexible and unstable as he is,
To come over to our faith.' There was a pause, then he added:

'The omniscient and omnipotent God knows that, were I without
A law, I would choose that law before all laws, and having once accepted it
Would strictly keep it.' Miramumelinus then inquired
What was the condition of this King of England and his kingdom;

To which Thomas, as the most eloquent of these messengers, replied:
'The King is illustriously and nobly descended from great kings,
And his territory is rich, and abounds with all kinds of wealth,
In agriculture, pastures and woods; and from it also every kind of metal

May be extracted by smelting. Our people are handsome and ingenious,
And are skilled in three tongues: the Latin, the French and the English,
As well as every liberal and mechanical pursuit. Our country, however,
Does not of itself produce any quantity of vineyards or olive trees,

But procures an abundance of these by trade from adjoining countries.
The climate is salubrious and temperate; it is situated between the west
And the north, and receiving heat from the west and cold from the north,
It enjoys an agreeable temperature. It is surrounded entirely by the sea,

Whence it is called the Queen of the Islands. The kingdom has, from times
Of old, been governed by an anointed king, and our folk are free
And manly, and acknowledge the dominion of no one except God.
Our church and the grace of our conviction is more venerated there

Than in any corner of world we know apart from there, and it is
Peaceably governed by the edicts of the Pope and of his Majesty.'
At the conclusion of this speech, the Emir heaved a sigh,
A deep sigh, and then replied: 'I never read or heard that any king

Possessing such a prosperous realm, subject and obedient to him,
Would thus voluntarily ruin his sovereignty by making tributary
A country that is free, by giving to a stranger that which is his own,
By turning happiness to misery, and thus giving himself up

To the will of another, conquered as it were without a wound.
I have rather read and heard that most would realise liberty
For themselves at the expense of streams of blood, which
Is considered praiseworthy. Now I hear though that your wretched lord,

A sloth and a coward, who is even worse than nothing, wishes, from
A free man to become a slave, who of all mortals is the most wretched.'
After this he asked, although contemptuously, what was his age,
Build and strength, and he was told that he was fifty, hoary in his mane,

Not lofty, but of compact size, and with a form appropriate for strength.
Here the Emir asserted, 'His youthful, manly vigour has fermented.
Now it begins to grow cool. Within ten years, if he lives that long,
His valour will fail him before he accomplishes any arduous enterprise.

That upon which he now resolves will fall into decay, good for nothing.
A man of fifty sinks, if imperceptibly: one of sixty visibly declines.
Better your king be at peace with himself, prepare for his demise.'
Again, he scanned the paragraphs, weighing up their pros and cons,

Then burst into a regal laugh sharp with indignation.
He rejected John's proposal with these final words:
'This so called king of yours is of no consideration.
He's nothing but a petty king, senseless, growing old. I care

Nothing about him. He is unworthy of any alliance.' Then,
Giving Ralph and Thomas his most baleful look, he says:
'Never come into my presence again, and may your kafir eyes
Never again behold my face. The fame, or rather infamy

Of that inept apostate, your master, instigates a stench obnoxious
To my nostrils.' Envoys out of favour, they backed away in haste,
But as they did, the Emir chanced to glance at Robert the clerk;
Least of these emissaries: a small man, dark, with one arm longer

Than the other, and having fingers all misshapen, namely
Two fused together, and with a face like a Jew. Thinking, therefore,
That such a contemptible looking person would not be sent to manage
A difficult business unless he were wise and clever, able to grasp

The nub of the matter, and noting by his cowl and his tonsure,
That here was a clerk in Holy Orders, he had him recalled;
For while the others had broached the appeal, Robert had stood silent,
Apart, at a distance. With these nobles gone, a private interview began,

The particulars of which the cripple later shared with his acquaintance.
Was King John a man of moral character, asked the Emir,
And did he have courageous sons and generative power?
He added, 'If you tell a lie, I'll not believe a Christian, if another

Comes my way, especially a clerk.' Robert, on his word, as a man
Of God, promised honest answers and affirmed that John
Was properly a tyrant not a king, known as a destroyer rather than
A governor, oppressor of his people, and leonine

Only as devourer of his subjects, while a lamb to foreigners,
And secretly allied to those who contended seemingly against him.
Had not his slothfulness cost him the Duchy of Normandy?
He was a loser of territory, and moreover eager to pillage

The kingdom of England – or to destroy it. How would he do it?
Why by extortion. He was an insatiable extorter. Extractor of the teeth
You need to eat. His own country's invader, eager to possess
His people's possessions. He had begotten few even adequate children,

Or rather none at all, but only such runts as took after their father.
He had a wife who was hateful to him and who hated him;
An incestuous, evilly disposed, adulterous beast of a woman,
Often found in flagrant dereliction of fidelity, on which the king

Would order that her paramours be duly seized and strangled on her bed.
Nevertheless, this self-same, so-called king was envious of his nobles
And relations, violated their marriageable daughters, and,
In his observance of his faith, was wavering and sceptic – 'As you've heard.'

When all this was taken in, the leader of the Saracens not only scorned
King John, just as he had before done, but also now detested him.
According to his own law, he cursed him, while demanding, 'Why,
Why do they allow such a criminal to reign, your wretched folk?'

Robert replied: 'The English may well be the most patient of men
Until they are offended and injured past endurance, my Emir.
But now, like a lion or that elephant he trumpets from at home,
When such a creature feels a hurt or sees its blood, it gets enraged,

And so the people rise, and are endeavouring, though late, to shake
The yoke.' The Emir blamed the too easy patience of the English, which
The interpreter, who had been attendant there, rightly attributed to fear.
Robert was then favoured by the Emir, and they conversed far more,

On many things, as Robert later told admiring friends. He then made
The clerk many costly gifts of gold and silver, jewels, silks and scents,
And bade him go in peace on friendly terms, whereas the other messengers
He neither saluted nor did he furnish with gifts as they departed.

On their return, they told King John all that they had heard and seen.
At which he wept in bitterness of spirit at being so detested
By this potentate, and at being thwarted in his aim. Robert however
Astutely regarded his Liege from all the foreign novelties

Bestowed on him, it being evident he had been received
More favourably than the others, though at first repulsed and kept apart.
On which account he was honoured more than they,
And, by way of reward, the King bestowed on him the charge

Of Saint Albans' abbacy, albeit this had never fallen vacant.
Thus was the clerk remunerated with the property of another.
Then, without consulting, yea, eke against the will of the incumbent,
Robert seized on every chattel held in that church and its convent.

Songs of Realisation

Epping – FIRST SONG OF REALISATION

Like an alphabet without letters, the lack of any difference
Between us implies that something you do where
You are doesn't enjoy an independent existence.
It's not easy to put Humpty-Dumpty together again,
So those impossible peacocks can only be an alternative
To the thorns among green fingers; but ask if there is one
Willing to transform its tail into a bridge or take the next
Porcelain step in their relationship. A prickly pear
May have its faults but still creates an arc of transference
Out of its prickles. Ask the peacocks. Unalike vibes produce
Unalike particle properties. You can't feel the inside of a cabbage.
Tiny crumpled dimensions can be instantaneously
Linked to something over there, regardless of distance.

Ask about the mouflon that raised their lyric horns among
Umbrella pines, thorns and shrubbery armed to the leaf;
Each of these a billion filaments of energy, unlike the town
Where death is unseen, age exiled, birth sequestered, love
Merely virtual. Gravity, general relativity, applies to big things.
Droppings like currants, and paths trodden by hooves
Are simply a cacophony of nonsense, cloud language,
Gutturals, sibilants and vocables, but never to hear one's
Native tongue or any other clearly is turning over an egg-timer
As you feel the changes to your velocity. The hairy snake
Can be scaled up – Tottenham compared to the bush of Epping.

For small things, there's a different 'superstring-speak'.
Vibration may not be the word. Fibrillation, fasciculation,
Tintinnabulation. Number language, fruit and veg language.

Polyglot Tottenham's a babble. Ruled rooves at the set angle,
Parallel ridges, brickwork. The high street calls for its *Lointain*:
Last summer it was southern Spain: lichen and the dried
Flambeaux of grasses seen on a wander. Spanish lavender,
Eagle owls and a stupa among the pines. This breezy day,
Luke Howard prompts us: 'Cumulus. Cumulo-nimbus.'
Ah, but there was smog back then. 'Tottenham International'
Cross-fades to a romantic vista on the edge of Woodford:
Not far away, yet remote as a Claude Lorrain.

Bark-plated pines in the south mustered behind
That mournful peacock calling beyond the density
Of bottle brush, savin bush, pistachios and butcher's broom...
Incense and myrrh. Bushes of *fines herbes*.
If only you knew which to chew for your pregnancy
Or for your varicose veins – or which not to touch.
Instead you spent a fair few hours trying to get shot
Of those nasty little prickles. Only by travelling light as
Down may we accept the way in which we drift
Through lives as if through landscapes on the air,
Finally settling, either to sleep or flower, where we are,
Or where we were when we saw that one enormous pine.

Further north, the trees develop goitres.
Yes, and threads that are there or not, as a breeze lifts a branch
At a sunbeam's touch. Forests are alive and dead.
Dying, they become their food. Petals like flattened pebbles,

Roots making veins in the path, and tracts of mire
You edge around, brushing things aside. For earth-encrusted
Uprootings visit High Beech: the elephants' grave-yard.
These once–airborne pachyderms have been laid low
By the hurricane. Here was a galleon. Now it's a hulk,
Its carcass prone against the slope. And no escape
From a pang of guilt. It's where I might have scattered mother;
Not where I did, within earshot of the motorway.
Mock the superstition of us atheists. Andrew, alert
For the third bloody magpie, veering off the central lane.

The bracken that we'd tunnel through, back then!
It was our own green ocean as the trees came into season.
Beech nuts carpeted well-spread stretches. Gone off the track
Into close-ups, we'd skirmish with holly and hazel.
Bridle paths ducked under fresh negligée foliage.
Dense rhododendrons bulged in barrowed clefts:
Clumps of these you could plumb to the depths,
Their hardened leaves to be pushed aside
Beyond those bracken seas – in Bear Wood – where
Each chamber denned in the heart of the thickets
Was private enough for the swapping of secrets
– And one who enters the forest intent on renunciation
May well be tempted by softness, mounds of delectable moss
Where springs originate, for the forest admits of opportunities,
Invites dalliance, releases its scents and flavours.
After all, its nature is to grow everywhere, to seed everywhere,
As well as to rot, decay and disintegrate.

          *   *   *

Here the hunt rides also, here things are killed and eaten,
All their remains gone over again, by ants, and again
By the mites that feed on *their* leavings. The forest
Laps at the fringes of our constructions, its birdsong
Drowned by the traffic, its thresholds clogged by garbage.
Choppers flutter overhead. The M25 now separates
Upshire and Boadicea's monument from reinforcing
Greenery. Planes drone like insects as they cross
Clearings of sky glimpsed through a spray of leaves.
Let's move away from the parking spot, getting into stride,
Overtaking other walkers waiting on their dogs.
Our destinations are circles: hikes that incorporate landmarks –
The Buddha tree, the inkpond, the camp.

In this built-up county now, the forest is a patch;
Though once the perilous everywhere else, reaching from
The dunes to the mountains: a vegetable Tsunami
Effortlessly smothering the isles of our urbanity.
Land's prevailing sea – of illusions formed from reality:
Death, disease, dissolution – fostering shoots and larvae,
Husks of things becoming loam like night.
Elsewhere there are werewolves and the misted retreats
Of the sages. Elsewhere there are chasms, table-fastnesses. . .
Unkempt hinterland hangs from unreachable heights
And chokes impenetrable depths. Elsewhere the bush is agog,
Its temples drowned in lianas, orchids and
Be-fronded cobras. Water-holes quench the jungle's thirst.
Steaming swamps fill a holy river's reaches.

What we've got, beyond the 406, are hillocks wrapped in copses,
Low-lying mire obstructing holly bottle-necks,

And tracts of heath, where, among clumps of furze,
Token cattle shake long horns at flies. A hidden golf-course
Backs away from birch, then oak, and then prodigious beech
– Seal-grey, lopped at antler-height, and squat,
Or left to soar above the make-shift graves
Hurriedly dug by near-by London's murderers
Behind those nettles ranked beside poached rides.
Deeper, an earthwork circles above its fosse
– Prohibited to boys on mountain bikes.

Here may be stumbled across the ingle of the gipsy witch,
And the lair of Turpin, rather than the glade of some Apsaras.
Here we have *our* wood-nymphs and the goblins
Who leer from our pollarded hornbeams. Are these
The cousins of those blue devils who prompted Clare
To commit himself to the forest's lunatic cell?
Remember, Tennyson lived here as well
At High Beech, delighted by the mad:
The most agreeable and the most reasonable
Persons he had met with. Did Clare discuss his hero
Wordsworth's words with him? Later there was trouble
At the asylum. Its founder Dr Allen's
Ecclesiastical sculpture nearly ruined Tennyson.
No more skating suavely over a frozen Connaught Water
Like a very yacht for grandeur, in his fine blue cloak.

Tennyson beat his retreat, and then, a year later,
Clare made good his escape. But you can find the forest
In his poetry. The 'brook without a bridge
And nearly dry' is Epping, where the brooks begin as
Runnels clogged with leaves. And Clare observed

The dogs that still get exercised 'where weeds
Are gifts too choice to throw away.'
But honestly, a forest's hornbeamed bogies
Can't be brought to book for a poet's instability.
Hard to discover a rickety bridge here
Or dine on a tile from a ginger-bread house.
Herne, you'll find, and a ragged-staff-brandishing bear.
It could be worse, be leshie, raksha, drude,
But then, there was that case – the 'babes in the wood'
And chauffeur-driven links to auctioned kids in Dolphin Square,
Or are these allegations we should disregard?
Just unsound inventions of a rumour-avid town
Whose Gherkin hives a forest-phobic populace:
Canary Wharfers, toasting to the Shard . . .

No need to invent those fish-net spangled birches
Flirting so seductively above their rooted boots.
Things are decidedly spooky. For instance, on magnetic
Hunter's Hill, you cannot tell if you're going up
Or if you're going down the slope, just as Turpin
Had no clue, as he rode for York, he rode *towards* the rope.
Farms well-placed for poaching fetched the highest rents back
then,
When pock-marked highwaymen handed ladies down
On the Cambridge Road. They'd split the loot
At Loughton Camp. A white hart was a sign to them.

*   *   *

Shifts of focus shudder the leaves that are strewn
In a seething carpet. Glare through the fork of a beech.
Wobbly humps? They're buried elephant trunks –
Those heffalumps that once were clouds. Look, he's got
A tusker on his head! A down of mildew forms on
One old stump. I went for a stroll here, once, with a girl
And there were these sea-cow faces. She looked ill,
And so did everything else. We photographed mushrooms,
Puffballs, moist cultures of mould, cumuli gone solid,
Slimy little oysters, toadstools emerging out of iridescent moss
In between the toes of dryads lightened of their shrouds.

But lift your eyes now. Climb to the brow of a hill,
Where, through the gaps, you can just get a glimpse
Of woodland stretching away to some smoky horizon.
Mythically forested distance. Leaves in their trillions, timber
Massed beneath; the game springing through thickets;
An endless labyrinth of ways, rooted sands, dips leading
Down onto rivulets bridged by rotting limbs, fairy rings
Encircling seedlings, honeysuckle bushes. Webs.
Berries. And cataracts that burst over ledges only
To plunge still deeper into the vaults of the wilderness.

Trees get seen through further when it's winter,
With nests among their tops; a sentinel crow, dark
As its perch. Watery woods, and a bruised overcast sky.
One very lofty evergreen in charge of hordes of forkeries...
Each naked tree divides and divides again
To splay its fan of twigs before the filigree of others
While ivy-mantled boles are lightning-blasted dignitaries,
Their gaunt gestures adding streaks of grey.

Brambles below remain vigorous, yes,
But the bracken's curling off into nothingness;
Just a few last ferns blenching in the sere blast.
Here a thistle remains, and deeper into the wood,
A trunk embedded in moss. Silver birch bark
Peels away from the mast. Trees with holes,
With navels torn, with burgeoning warts, with bristles.
Foliage burnt by autumn now a mulch.
Slippery logs and leaf-drifts clog the gullies.
Hoary sinews choke the oaks, bind their limbs
And bring them down, while a slope's up-ended beeches
Sprawl with their root-balls ripped out and exposed.
Ever too shallow a grip on the sandy soil of Essex.

Now the clouds are very low; the ponds here frozen over.
Come New Year, the forest may well be swathed in snow:
Holly sprigs covered in icing, the stuff clinging to the north
Of trunks, trapped in forks, weighing down the evergreens
Or evidencing tracks, and the birch looking slightly soiled,
Compared to this bright, immaculate carpet.
Brush past a branch and release a shower of flakes.

Forest cloaked in silence. An alb thrown over its gurning.
A crepe bandaging those ulcers in the bark;
Blanketed gargoyles eating off platters of fungi,
The fluff trying its best to plug splintered-off torsos,
Scars, rents in the fabric. Spite of attempts at a hospital whiteness,
Everywhere are innards still exposed, casings flipped askew:
Essays in mortality augmented by the forest's imagination.

*   *   *

This winter, as the sun begins to set,
A seemingly motionless jet
Floats above the lake, while chevrons to the south
Beat their way across a pristine sky.
A helicopter with one flashing light hovers over the trees.
These surround a feathered shore. Duck-shit and dead leaves.
Mud and rot in the nostrils. Mess at the water's edge.
The afternoon is cold and clear; the blue, pale ceramic
Infused with a faint pink stain. Islands belonging to birds
Breed dreams of pirate hideaways. You feel what's underneath
In the soles; a tract of sludge, then gravel, roots and stones.

As the sun enters the lake, a plaintive moorhen
Sounds a knelling note. Withered sedge. The lakeside damp,
With leaves on the sod going darker than brown.
There's a fissure in the trunk of that corpse
Which bends forward in admonishment perhaps,
Rising like an omen out of undergrowth. Everywhere
The woods approach, and geese honk and duck quack.
Magpies and crows pace the land, while from the lake
A splash now, a brookish babble, strangled squeak
And klaxon hoot. And then there is the increasing
Splutter and rush of take-off. Tails wag. Bottoms up.
Rustle of rats and voles in rushes. Patterns play
On the shivering surface: widening circles, arrows.
Rotted innards freeze as the winter tightens its grip.
Time for hibernation and retreat – but not for ducks,
Not for whatever screeches from the twigs.

The underground exposed, the overhead submerged;
The living interred and the buried re-appearing.

Red ripples cross the black shallows. Beyond,
There's a darker ink to the depths. The trees are arterial webs,
Delicate as coral in the enlarging glow. Again, there's a violent
Beating – rapid approach from a neighbouring inlet.
The neck is spear or trumpet, sounding its attack.
As this aggression is acted out, the cover thickens
Into night while embers glow within the water.
Stains of lichen deepen ashore. Distant flocks wheel tighter
Then come banking into spray. Crested and be-ruffed,
The duck drift closer to the sluice. Branches dip into reflections.
The shadow of the wood is encroaching on the sunset.
And sunset striped with silhouettes engenders fearsome tigers:

Tigers that slide through a forest from which
The night never departs. Evergreen night below the Himalayas;
Utterest dark its natural pelt; its fastnesses like dungeons;
Its pines erect; each needled bough secreting a tart odour.
Those that are felled will be contested. Mountainous
Taiga is sacred; massed against the brink of crags;
Nourishing the cordyceps and shading the azalea.
Wild legions of spruce. Chir pine, laurel and juniper,
Stands of fir and widening sweeps of cedar.
All sorts of spiky Chinese conifer. Night woods,
Where we venture in to milk it of its turpentine –
The terebinth – bleeding the trunk, or at least,
Making it ejaculate. Or do people get high on it?

Scales compacted, ripening its male or female seeds,
Cone-like consciousness expands and opens to release these.
The shape of the pineal gland resembles both the clitoris
And a cone. Located at the centre of our brain,

This primal eye belongs to our earliest Self.
It opens in his trance, with his seed about to spill
As the civet cat its spray, as the terebinth its resin.

Holly as ever stiff in the leaf, waxed to its spikes,
Indomitable, and wound about his antlers by the shaman:
He who can cure the headaches of elephants, woader
Of spirals and whorls, crescents, worms and the eyes of wolves,
With din drums to beat out the trances that dream up
The universe in the heads of foxes: many paws go dangling
From his groin. Renewing his strength in the instant
That he spends it, yet with the force of a thwarted urge,
He loiters in the pinewoods, poaches the verderers' wives,
And loses his lingam in order that it may become
A universal promise of fertility, priapic wand and axle
Of infinity. All generation and seeding comes to a stop
Then quickens in the winter's heart. Stretched across zero,
His drum-skin vibrates – the universe being that membrane.
So he makes a ring of stars: his drum creates creation
With the same step as his flame reduces it to ashes.

The instant passes. 'Now we are gamut and fulcrum
Joined in the clinch of space and time – game of a god
With his consort. Whenever we tremble with passion
The whole foundation trembles. Terrible omens arise –
A rain of bloody bones comes down, fierce winds blow,
Comets fall, and no one reads the Vedas. Once we created
Creatures prone to immortality: creatures like ourselves,
Blazing, blazing with energy, carrying skulls and drinking Soma,
Their seed drawn up in chastity, each having thousands of eyes,
Of such terrible gaze no one could look upon them:

Great tigers of great power – projecting endless desire.
Now, though, we undo desire by giving you the enjoyment:
Drink, and thirst is gone; spout, and spouting's done.'

All over the earth, as the sun goes down,
Lakes and ponds turn gold. A flaming drop has entered them.
Molten water matches sky and the clouds like islands
Floating there, while islands nesting underneath
Are clouds adrift on flame. Rings where a duck has dived
Or a fish has leapt interconnect as a female sun
Tosses her last wild locks at the night. Then serpents
Writhe across silver. Deer come to drink. And a tiger
Crouches by the bank, lapping up the moonlight.

Chauvet – SECOND SONG OF REALISATION

Someone is digging a hole by the Charing Cross Road.
Pedestrians edge past orange hurdles. Cables inside coils
Are exposed, and a length of rope is being used,
Possibly to extract something from somewhere else.
They have dug several feet down, so far, between
Large and small manhole covers. Four parallel pipes
Can be seen – they must run along underneath the pavement.
They have opened up this hole by slicing through
Previous patch-ups, cutting into the first thin layers
Of the twentieth century. Kattwinkel's butterfly
Led him over the edge of time. The sun is out, and your shadow
Falls into the hole. He fell three million years
And landed in the Olduvai. Hand-axe, hand-grenade, mobile...
Oldowan tools are two hundred and sixty thousand generations
Past their best for purpose date. They have been supplanted
By the middle and the upper Palaeolithic, the Mesolithic
And the Neolithic ages, then by the age of copper,
Bronze, iron, steel and microchip. Time is a frozen river
In which those rough-hewn flints are suspended forever.
When you click on tools, your action is cast on the future.
Kattwinkel's butterfly floated over an abyss.

But now you enter my home page to click on contact.
I am on heat and the clammy folds of my sides
Are warmed by the drumming, the trance and the shaman's urine.
Bong goes the calcite gong, bong, as the frozen drip of time
Gets repeatedly struck. They unroll a plastic strip
To form a track, for the floors are as rich as the walls.
The layout they establish inserts a double-click access denied

E-bay search. Your new search saves are of sites:
Homo Heidelbergensis, Chauvet, the Olduvai Gorge.
Each is temporarily edited on the net with bookmarks
To help you survive in the least visited domains. You substitute
Add-ins for mailings, erase dinosaur pop-ups.
You view gridlines and zoom onto split thumbnails.
You penetrate my text to cut and paste. You delete
Everything in the draft layout of my document, replacing it
With a crudely explicit message. Time is a frozen river,
And in it the early hominids are under pressure
Not to co-operate with each other, even though
It may be in their own best interests to do so.

Better words are needed. Each of your families clings
To its own lingo, and so you will never agree on the thing
By name alone. But you can agree *if you see* that the biggest thing
About the thing is its head, and this is a hairy-hided one
Impervious to arrows, and you can see that on either side
Of what some call its pipe, this has two long hooks.
You must club together now, since you are agreed
That here is the thing as it looks. Then you should dig its bed in me,
Spread this with a coverlet of green overlaid with ochre
So that it looks firm. And many hunters will be needed,
Yours and theirs and others, all your allies. You will bed
The hook-thing down. After all, his hooks are older than
Our mushroom mother figurines; indeed, the breasted ones
Are sometimes made of him: things as worn by
Service within as the smooth tool, the master-pin.
The hook-thing stamps and noises – you must charm him.
He must fall in love with you, for only thus
Will you bed him. Charm his master, charm him too,

Making sure that your poems avoid all metrical clichés,
Your footwork is original, your drumming springs surprises.
Cracks, caverns, and tunnels are the entrances
To the interior of hills rising like storm-clouds out of the bush.
They lead you to the yawning malocas of the animals.
There, within their interior, the gigantic prototypes
Of each species exist, their progeny folded inside them.
Twitter, screech and whistle, for the hills know what you mean.

*   *   *

Mimetic learning of predator avoidance is also
Widespread, and 'here too we can readily appreciate
That individual trial-and-error learning of the behavioural
And dietary profile of other species is likely to be
An inappropriate and costly strategy.' My maharaja
Dances, then he does it . . . The earth moves,
And within my depths one pendulous concretion falls.
Calcite lands on dank rock and shatters in a flash:
Smashed spray of glitter-seeds that skitter across
A limestone floor, just as an avalanche from above the tree-line
Bursts on a valley in spring, splintering pine; or pods crack,
Or brash lightning strikes, or pounded vines engender
Dancing stars. You fizz now with the minutiae of beginnings:
Pollen, sand, smoke, sperm, very small seeds, the Milky Way,
Fish-spawn in a stream, the grain of wood and the pores
Of your skin. Mammoth booms and pygmy pings
From litophonic drops play bagatelle among the spots
Blotted near my resonance point – maràri dots
Come quickly here, but nothing stirs the ursine
Hibernation. For man comes only in summer,

Leaves a winter cave to hairier scratchers – artists
With big claws. Migration wings man south, seeking warmth.

Put your ear to the ground. Sense on your cheek
The slightest draught escaping from the scree
Or a breath discerned through the entrance to a fox's earth.
It is thus you detect the secret ear of the hill,
And then the first sighting of calcite draperies, and drawings so old
You're deep beneath Holborn. The cavalcade of adverts
Demands your attention. Changing onto the Jubilee,
You find yourself descending into a Piranesi,
Chipping away at the words, retouching their edges.
Basically you're only down here in order to emerge
Somewhere else. But say there's delay? Go down, deeper,
Drop to the slow, local axis, where time takes
Longer to pass than on some mountain-top. Not still,
Exactly, but ever so slow, rotating so that
What branches above must gather speed, flailing
To keep up. Himalayas, clouds … These undergrounds
We travel through are not the cave, for the cave is a place.
It takes us nowhere, not from place to place. In time, perhaps…
And we shall only abandon it to follow the tundra as it
Recedes, or stay with the herds that head south.

The lines in the wall, the lines in the palm, the lines
Of the paw that follow the fissure's contour. Then stencils
And prints. You have lifted your child so his hand
May touch my roof, to make an impression, for luck.
The uniform shape of the hand-axe over space and time
Speaks of a tradition, while hefty cobbles – portable quarries,
Grindstones, anvils – near a dry lake in Australia –
Are proof of an expanding social vista. You are more adept

At speed through space by now, but here you need to travel back
And back and back, deeper into the cave, beyond
The nests of bears. Irregular shaft of the path within –
But there is an inside to the walls inside, there is
Another side to them. As the membrane of the vagina
Feels, from within, your penetration, so the walls of the cave
Feel the drops that touch them, the spots, the hands,
The sprinkling of powder that leaves the silhouette
With its span spread, feels the fragments of bone you press
Into its crevices, feels the image as it emerges
From the phosphines you project upon it, feels the aurochs,
The rhino, the lion, there, there on its hide, the image from within,
As a hand grasps the hand-axe. The inside of a cave
Is just an inner skin, receptive as a perianth of petals.
Yes, within the rock, there is a listening.

*   *   *

I am your woman, your screen. I am your web, your net.
Surf me as you would your private files and favourites.
I feel you in the depths, in the entrails; but also in the stars
Gazing so steadfastly down. On the earth, and below the earth,
And above the earth. Earthquakes, landslides, volcanoes.
And we are obsessed by what is beneath us, by caves,
By crypts and bunkers, war-rooms; cellars, mines and tombs.
Time is a frozen river, and somewhere along it the tube
Moves with sealed doors along the inside of another tube.
Wheels below this floor go trundling along the rails.
'Alight here for the British Museum' – above him
The Rosetta Stone adds weight to the mass of London.
Burrowing beneath the town he threads a maze of tiles,

Tarmac floors, underground passages, shafts, escalators, ledges,
His target a profound hammam – sauna and massage –
Below a public library. At Grimes Graves they mined the flint:
Flint or quartz or antler tine for hammering the core.
Axe polished smooth on grinding stone. Debitage
Of broken flakes. It was between five and two and a half
Million years ago that we took up the stone, found it misshapen
And gave it an appropriate symmetry, a symmetry
We saw around us: in the limbs of creatures, in our eyes
And nipples, in reflections, quartz – as in seasons, years.

The females are more gracile, but these ones are not of your breed,
Nor of the breeds to which you are allied. Groan of brakes,
Wheeze of sliding doors, roar of ventilation. Females
Blur their estruses, thus inducing a situation
Of scramble competition between males. But social
Organisation is unexcavatable. It is quite possible
That all the interpretations are hopelessly wrong,
And in any case, we shall never know which of them are correct.

Inhale the steam. Relax. Allow your state to change.
The interior of the cave invites you to think outside your head,
Your Palaeolithic monitor. The 'Power-law' may be female coercion
Through ritual regulation of sexual access, just as the source
Of Soma, nectar of the gods, may be a woman who rises nude
From the waist up from the roots or trunk of the birch,
Her breasts swollen with milk for anyone who approaches her.
Great ardour grows where the bat-dung drop
Splatters in the midst of a hexagonal. I am the web of the world.
Spider and weaver of the universe. Shiva ejaculates a rainbow.
The shaft of the Master of Animals constitutes a shaft in my interior.

The knowledge referred to is as a poker cooled in the pond.
Sexual knowledge is as a comet cooled in the ocean.
Fiery semen cooled in the Ganges has the potentiality
To enable his demons to attain that force which has reached
A level of excess and threatens destruction. Oölitic stone
Resembles the roe of a fish. Her head resembles the cap
Of a mushroom. Shape me, I am limestone to your flint.
Black nodular flint. For lustre, and for ease of flaking.
Tap, chip, retouch, peck. Product of mysterious silica
Found in chalk deposits dating from the upper cretaceous:
Melt-down from the internal skeletons of sponges,
A mobile, gelatinous mass. Light grey, speckled, boulder-clay
Flint demonstrates the difference in ripples of percussion.
Patina of chalk. Denticulate chip. Many of the nodules
Are termed 'paramoudra' flints. Indicating bioturbation,
They're the negative space of an animal's cave. For these
Nodular flints are trace fossils of the burrows of an unknown
Organism. Because it is known only by its trace, both trace
And creature share the same name. We do not know much about
Flint, still less about *Bathicnus paramoudrae*, a creature
Only guessed by her abode. The tuberous eidonomy of a flint
Indicates the internal space of a dwelling. Did she have
Powerful hands? Patrol her residence for worms?
Not a gregarious being, tunnel for herself alone? And did he
Tunnel towards her, rapidly, below the turf, in order
To fulfil their rapture, the mole's ancestor? Pushing the earth up
Out of her home, the equivalent of you pushing a
Reluctant elephant out of a hole with a hand, the hand
Which holds the stone at which you aim a blow. Indirect percussion
Calls for antler tines, and leaves exhausted cores and burins.

What Eve offered him was autopoiesis – bitter fruit –
The thought of self-creation. Eve said, 'Suppose
That you made me, made this apple and yourself.' The tree
Of knowledge had its roots in power; initially the power
Of retention. Determined to manipulate both nature and society,
It grew as a tree that would build itself rather than flower.
It was this will to dominate that annoyed Jehovah enough
To cast them out, for the knowledge that man is made
In God's image poses an ovate question. It is thus that a creature
Usurps the role of creator. Thus the shaman made off with
The elixir – yes, and once this occurred, our extended
Residency in the garden was over. Man, the original sin
Was to sense that God might be made in your image.
Ultimately, the shaman assumed immortality and became lost
– Seeking a goal, he blazed a trail through the jungle
And the jungle died. At last he came to the still battlefield
Over which the winter of time had passed. Here he picked up
A flake knapped from Langdale tuff. Our hundred
Thousand-year primacy poses a threat to the balance of the closed
Universe. We have lost sight of our niche. No thread
Of light through the dark. Larger groups tend to be unstable.

He had forgotten his role as a drinker of poison
With serpents which serve as adornments; wise one,
Guardian of game, spirit of each meeting stream;
A dancer and his consort who enjoyed the drops
That soaked them in the heat of the monsoon.

They welcomed the scents, the hands, the sprinkling
Of powder, the offering that was the smoke;
A pair who were time and eternity; a pair who would feel it
A curse to hurry the sunrise or restrain the sunset.
Where are they now? Their shrine is dry and untended.

The vines hide it from view
Around the back of a yellow-walled hotel.
To penetrate further into the cave is to walk forwards in time.
The present is found where the drawings are deepest.
Scan the deepest drawing and you grasp what's going on:

Belted rhinoceros contests – the betting is heavy,
The hunting in prides: here imitation pays.
Size may equate with quantity. Three years ago,
A large herd of reindeer. Last year the herd was small.
This year lions, and no reindeer at all.

*   *   *

Verdigris of lichen on late winter branches.
In the dimension of trees – in the wide forest of the mind –
He is having intercourse with the undergrowth.
There is a wood inside his cave. The world grows warmer,
And the forest encroaches on the tundra. The forest
Smells of woman. The drop echoes through limestone curtains.
The cave smells of bear. The sound of the tundra is of hooves.
Zillions of strings connect the sun to our earth.
Birds pour scorn on your headgear. Sniff the air.
Scent of flowers, odour of pollen, acrid stink of ants,
Whiff of fungi, sweet perfume of ripeness, musky

Spray of rutting beasts, stench of rotting fruits and
Decaying leaves. Courtship and preening, sniffing and licking.
I am the cave. Inseminate me. My echoing depths awake
The chords of an arcane lullaby. On the jewelled isle
Which is also the cave of origins, I am the energy of the drop.
The red god dances within me. Shiva dances within me,
The shaman dances within me. The self-awakened
Rests on his comatose twin: I use them both as my divan.
They were originally me, for I am the whole of being,
Shiva is the conscious self, while Shava sleeps beneath him.
But I am the all of what there is: that larger thing than self,
I am that which self inhabits: a space in between the stilt-roots;
The interstices, hollows, holes, the underneaths and groins:
Home for snakes and toads, for spiders, scorpions, voles,
And, in the wet, minnows and crabs. I am this dark
And humid tangle of spiny conductors. Region of creases, conduits,
Bifurcations. I am which came first. I am your inner bath:
A pool covered with lotuses. I am the nurturing bear,
And therefore I am a notion fuelled by accelerating change
In the development of wealth, technology and your capability
For information processing. Extrapolating these capabilities
To the future, it is feasible to envisage the emergence of
A self-improving artificial breast or mother-intelligence
That is so much beyond present capabilities that it becomes
Impossible to understand it with today's conceptions.

But look at the man who once had a river run through him,
Whose head was full of trees. Nature used to permeate his body.
A lizard would crawl up his back. Serpents slept in the bowl
Of his pelvis or swayed. The plants were inside him,
Their smells were his words, their leaves his ideas.

His toes contained little tubers, the clinging vines were his fingers.
When he saw stars the cave would flower. The spots
Would coagulate into bison, the stone would drip with desire.

Back in those days he just grabbed her and dragged her
Back to his cave. In those days it didn't matter
That she was a Neanderthal. All that mattered was lightning,
Ejaculation, causing the blossoms to fall, the seed-pods
To explode, the crystals to shatter. But even then a separation
Of roles was an advantage, enabling binary specialisations
To flourish. Today he retreats in the face of youth,
Slinks to his lair like a sick dog, to be alone with his age.
Dismal, he sinks in his own marshes, gets sucked
Into himself, goes under. He has been inside an anaconda.
He has been vomited out, a bag of evil-smelling bones.
Watch him as he logs in, goes to his home-page. No new messages.
A wink or two from a cam girl. That bare bottom
Is a hooker; that bit on the side, a hyena. His own messages
Have not been opened by the relevant bipeds. He trawls through
The sites again. This week's featured primates include Diane,
Glam orang-utan, 49, looking for discrete no strings fun
With adventurous gorillas of any race, age or colour,
And Hi, we R outgoing, love 2 laugh, love meeting new gibbons.
Tyne and Wear though's a distance, and so is Strathclyde.
Emma has kissed a few frogs in her life and would like to meet a prince.

Street-level stratus – call it fog. The dampness winds
Its way around the calves, the waist, the throat. My bed
Needs that Habitat rug. Winter has decided to stay.
Sky rises from the ground up, grey and pretty solid.
Uniform dullness augers a bad start to the day
When plug prompts no spark, and Lindi has to get up
In the dark to prepare her lesson plans. In 1826
The pea-soup in the city was 'as dense as we ever
Recollect to have known it. Lamps and candles
Were lighted in all shops and offices, and the carriages
In the street dared not exceed a foot pace.
At the same time, five miles from town, the atmosphere
Was clear and unclouded, with a brilliant sun.'
That was Tottenham then. Crepuscular light
Instils a warmth through subterfuge and sodium.
The cold that makes me wish never to end my hibernation
Emanates from the sky. The damp is made of the sky.
The drizzle is part of it too. Packets of hot gas
Should perform this meditation at the three twilights.
But the weather goes from bad to worse again.
I wield the flail of the lashing hail. Rain and the blast
Remind us how his fury that others have presumed to fill
Creation to the brim while he was under the sea
Causes him to become the destroyer as well, but this
Enables creation to emerge as a process, since without death –
Which he provides – the universe cannot replenish itself –
Just becomes packed with Helium, Hydrogen, Methane,
Isotopes and boundless modes of vibration: an immeasurable
And dense proliferation of possible branches

Plus the atomic number Z. The sharing of electrons
Between atoms and the way matter absorbs or emits radiation
Suggests that perhaps God does enjoy Roulette.
Whether by chance or not, eventually a ball will roll into the slot.

How nice it would be, though, to stay in the cave
And go on burrowing into your woman.
Think of her in the form of the syllable Om.
She resembles molten gold, is adorned with jewels,
And bedecked with parijatam flowers. Waters
Which descend on the heart thunder in its cavities
As the deep pools below falls effervesce with
The cataclysmic impact of a blooming nebula
On spectral lines and song lines. Clouds underwater.

Swimming or flying through these, your inner feats
Are one stage above the nearly vegetable state
Of the passive one who lies underneath; the id or less,
Mere 'beingness', at the very bottom of that pile
Presided over by our fierce mother. Stratocumulus clouds
Present their cotton scoops in an elongate form,
And through them you look down on ripe gardens,
Temple-roofs, fountains babbling murmurously and forever.
A snakelike thing, over the land you meander,
Creating rivers, waterways and lakes: 'daughter
Of earth and water, and the nursling of the sky...'
And chance has a lot to do with it, I'd say:
The Brownian motion of pollen specks on the surface
Of a pool, but others see it another way when sunbeams
Are admitted into a building and shed light on its shadowy places.

Witness in the beam a multitude of tiny particles mingling
In a multitude of ways. Their dancing indicates underlying
Movements that are hidden from our sight and originates
With atoms; for, set in motion by the impact of their invisible
Blows, miniscule compound bodies in turn cannon against
Slightly larger ones and gradually this jostling emerges
To the level of our senses, which move of themselves,
Making sense of it all, while themselves compounded of
Multitudes of tiny particles that ricochet through
The matter of which they are made. 'I pass through the pores
Of the ocean and shores; I change, but I cannot die,'
Says Shelley's cloud, and we have no more density than these.

*   *   *

For though each cell in the human body contains
About a hundred times as many atoms as there are stars
In the Milky Way, the nucleus of each atom
Is as a pinhead surrounded by eight-hundred metres of dust motes.
That atom is just so much space. Flint is just so much space.
Matter, just so much space. Mind is so much space.
But what fills space, if anything? Emptiness, I disown.
I sit beneath the fig, look upwards at the sun,
Gazing through a leaf as I turn brown.
From some other view, the leaf is simply green;
From underneath, a filigree of tributaries, a delta flooding
Backwards on itself, feeding on light while drinking moisture.
Eyesight ploughs through granules of time, or rather
My view, from below, of the leaf, comes wading towards my retina.
Figment of light from the sun above, wading through granules
Of space, as the leaf lifts in the breeze and fields of viridian energy

Flow through me, through the leaf and through the sun,
Connecting every grain of me with every single thing;
With every line attached to the elsewhere; the one
Thus being as multiple as any wave is a particle.
So emptiness is largely metaphysical;
Illusory, but lovely, as you pause, consider, reflect
On the rest at the end of some intricate passage.
Emptiness being a sort of bliss, as expressed
By Barnet Newman perhaps, or Morandi,
Or by a dense bouquet of clouds by Fantin-Latour:
Roses, leaves, bowl and background, all of the same matiére.

We are made up of clouds, those fleets of white barges,
Those patron goddesses of idle men. Purpose means nothing,
But, equally, purposelessness means nothing.
We are moved in much the same way as photons
Collide with electrons. That motion that we see in sunbeams,
Is our own, for we too are driven by blows that remain invisible.
In this dreaming lies the sacredness of the earth.
For singing up the country makes it come up quicker;
That is, come into existence, seeing as to exist is to be perceived,
As it is for quanta. Room for more in the carbon shell –
While the pursuit of analogy led us to fracture
Flint into a flake with scallop-shape. Electron shells
Prefer life filled or empty but get uneasy coaxed into states in between.
Galaxies collide near the wish-fulfilling kalpadruma tree.
A green beech holds up a grey oak with her arms.
Corpuscular light may ripple as well as an animal's flank,
And a crowded nucleus set the scene for a densely inhabited shell.
Within this cloud of electrons, how tough it is to think
Of things inconceivably smaller than the imperceptibly small.

One conceivable snowdrop has been out for a week,
The crocuses are looking up. A little shoal of cirro-cumulus
Floats in the Cambridge blue mocking Oxford spires.
The smeary disk that's ablaze in the north-east
Can't be looked at without a stain burning into the cornea.
Light-suffused vapours move beneath it, below the brim
Of my cap, wafting past a weather-vane with a bull
Balanced on top of it. While noting this, the shoal I saw
Has drifted behind St Aldates, for the sky
Is seldom still. Just for now, a crest provides
A backdrop to the aerated spire below the bull.
Pigeons are here and there. The blue is almost a glare.
Lighter here than the sea, this will eventually deepen
Into azure then darken as it fills with the ubiquitous
Pollen of the universe, the sprinkling of photons
With microwaves in the background. 'Tell you what
To do with the vicar, hang the bastard up on a coat-hanger!'
Mutters the mendicant sharing the bench with me
As the chimes coincide with the quarter in Carfax tower.

The mind must be clear as the sky, and yet
There is something of a coat-hanger about the Scales;
The sky of course being full of names. The daytime ones,
Luke Howard coined: names intended as terms
For the structure of wraithlike forms, the meaning of each
Carefully fixed by a definition in Latin. Why?
Because your local terms 'take away from the nomenclature
Its present advantage of constituting a universal language,
By means of which the intelligent of every country
May convey to each other their ideas.' Howard never
Named the vapour trail which now bisects the gap

Between BHS and Primark – gone by the time
I have written this down. It was a painting on water,
As Robert's weeping water faces evaporate before done
On the rock he is painting them on. The day ends
In a fiery Götterdammerung... Furious cloud at sunset.
Violet flowers unfurling in the west, tossed on their stalks
As blood gets spilt on the arras, while darkness seeps out
Of the ground and wells up into the trees. Roots
Become branches at night as the sky fills with earth...

*   *   *

We call white horses 'grey'. When my unsaddled one
Rolled above Uffington, clouds were all that filled
Each rolling eye. Vaporous shapes, ever-changing, adrift.
We had ridden there by bridle path; along the Thames
And then through beech woods, onto the old roads
Meeting up with the Ridgeway: a ride that leads on
Into the sky: parallel lines of cart-ruts taking us
Chalkily up and over the downs, their verges
Flanked by flinty fields or seas of bearded barley,
Hawthorn dips and clumps on crests: Whitnam,
And Wayland's Smithy. Clouds of white blossom
Billowing out from the cooling towers of Didcot.
Yes, and the sky is filled with tracks, and the straight
High tracks of England string our rings together
As the song-line strings together dreamings and sings up
Landmarks, and as we've cast our lines among
The stars and strung together their clusters,
Each configuration being a walkabout, a voyage;
And since the last word of its song coincides

With the very last step of your walk for all its reams,
The song is like a telescope, it allows the singer to see
Along the line, beyond the line of sight, beyond multiple
Horizons – and plumbs the depths of an ancestor's dreams.

Lying on one's back, one knee up, hands behind the head,
Admiring the poised euphuisms, the mares' tails –
Fair weather forms with firm seams perhaps,
Risen on thermals from the sun-warmed sea,
Their heads beginning to dissipate as the day cools
And to spread along the horizon with golden outlines
To their crests – you might consider their silence, and how,
As they float like rests across the stave of a starry night,
They assist the music of the spheres. Melodies
That accompany the Odysseys of Aboriginal hikes
Illustrate the actions of the feet: a slurred phrase
For a salt-pan slog, a cadence for the threading
Of a creek. 'Spinifex', 'Ant-hill' 'Mulga-scrub'.
Music can serve as a memory map. To find our way about,
We will pluck notations from the wheeling constellations
And weather-lore from some old ballad line:
'I saw the new moon late yestreen with the old moon in her arm...'

In the ensuing storm, a white horse jumps from a seething sky
Onto the hill above Uffington manger, flung up from the deep
Along with a cow and the moon, as gods and demons
Churn the milky ocean, using the cosmic serpent as a rope.

They have wound his scaly trunk round and round
Mount Meru which pivots on its axis in outer space
On top of the shell of a tortoise, and the devis cling to its tail
Refreshed by ocean breezes, while the demons have its head.

They send the universe into a spin as the serpent's breath
Turns hot and foul and the demons flag, debilitated:
Titans, fallen angels, ogres and corrupted nymphs
Gasping for air, and thirsting, thirsting for the ambrosial

Drink they will share with the gods, once it appears
On the surface, which is why they think it a good idea to have
Agreed to join forces. Ah, but the gods are cheats;
The horde of ghouls and goblins, rejects and wrong turns

Ought to have guessed they'll get none of it. First, though,
A poison wells up, as with the narcotic brewed from
The udder of a star-capped fly agaricus. Shiva gulps this down
While Parvati, anxious, takes him by the neck and squeezes.

Now she glances at the wish-fulfilling tree, which the tug-of-war
Has also flung up as well as a four-tusked elephant.
She wishes for an antidote – the poison only harms his throat,
And gratefully now he places the Pleiades around hers.

      *   *   *

Their sky is peopled with bears, and, from this sparkling cloud,
The stars that fell in the night onto the mushroom's hood
– White spots on red ground – are expressed in subterranean
Depths by red spots on grey stone: negative vision

Appropriate for a cave. The spots amount to animals
As those on a jaguar's jerkin indicate the stars.
Spring is in the night which is full of brilliant crocuses.

Jaguar swallowed the moon. With a pair of bellows
Or with pursed lips the gusts of March blow things awry...
The clouds race away, and for once there's a clear night sky.
Somewhere above, the Archer aims at the sea-goat,
His arrow that of time. Here and there a satellite
May be spied on its voyage across this ocean of ink.
Look for a triangle of dim stars – this is the upper part
Of the scales that connect the two asymmetrical balances
That sail across the waters of existence, with decks twinkling –
Like on some liner where a gambler with infinite capital
And infinite time on his hands is making one of an
Infinite number of wagers. Scorpios hangs close to the horizon.
Orion limps across the dark. Aries looks nothing like a ram.
One familiar ladle swings around the northern pole.
And the great square of Pegasus gives us a line on Arcturus.

You only need look up on such a night,
To get into the beyond and the notion of the beyond
Beyond the beyond. Outer space, or at least a decent view of it,
Would have appealed to Claude, for it is the epitome
Of yearning, of the faraway, of wonder, and a sense
Of immensity and its indifference. A map of the night is
A map of time. It provides us with the terrain
Into which the pharaohs have vanished, likewise
The Victorians, having lost their legs,
And as for the Americans, they're running
Out of lubricant, influence, impressiveness and capital,

And in general there have been as many empires
As there have been hair-styles, and were we out there,
It would be sublime, though sublime only in thought,
So far as the planets go, viewed from below
In Tottenham, where one seldom sees through
The city's glare anything more than a sheet of nimbostratus.

However, darling, when you dance, the force you feel
If you spin is proportional to the amount of matter
In the universe. And out there, as it seems, *among* the stars
In the comparative shallows, as it were, suspended by
Just the same forces, and within reach of our pull,
A silver tube yaws several degrees in order to incline
Towards the designated galaxy. Bright as a fish, it floats
Far above cirrus, above the last blur of the atmosphere,
A lid held up above its eye. It can look back to the source
Of the frozen river. Thirteen, fourteen, fifteen billion years...

Steadily, serenely, it bounces the light that hits its
Primary mirror onto its convex secondary one,
Then back through a hole in the first onto
Its focal point: generally powered by Phoebus,
Its optics mediated by instruments using complex
Filters to screen out different types of ray
While capturing light from the universe
And converting it into digital data for earth
And the space station, and for the world wide web.
Turbulence in our atmosphere causes the stars
To ripple, but the tube suspended in space,
Flanked by solar arrays and communications
Antennae, is above all that – for glinting in

The dark of our shadow or lost in a dazzling halo,
This is the current best for purpose tool
To evolve out of our quest to locate ourselves
With sextants, compasses and glasses.
What is the smallest stellar pinpoint its
Resolving power is capable of picking out?
How close together can two objects get and still
Be read as a pair? Hubble can see detail down
To less than 0.1 of an arcsecond across – this
Is ten times clearer than a telescope on earth.
It swims like a pilot fish around us
– Orbiting in about an hour and a half.

*   *   *

Hubble's airless eye allows us all to peer
Into solar systems turning like immense gyroscopes
Around their suns; deeper shells and wider rings;
Flashes creating light echoes, dwarfs that suck in
Giants; vast galactic crashes and star-forming nurseries
With at least ten dimensions to their pens:
Up and down, ahead and back, inside outside,
Outside in, clockwise, anti-clockwise,
Over-towards and under-towards, right way up
And upside down, back then and up ahead,
Before ahead and after back, above now and below it –
Each dimension matched by its opposite;
Nebulae twisted together in braids or shaken loose
In light-suffused auras, colliding spirals
Or even the three-branched creeper of Messier 83.

Lenticular, elliptical, even irregular galaxies
– Intricate whorls – as if tattooed on a shaman.
Yet the symmetry we aimed for in the flint
Underpins the laws of at least this local universe:
It's just nature's way of keeping everything from
Happening all at once. We shouldn't lose track
Of the horizon problem as we surmise
That everything rushing away may nevertheless connect,
But there's no getting away from the fact
That we're all tied to the apron-strings of our origins.
Indeed we now conjecture that a single species of string
Could execute a number of vibrational patterns –
Each the song of an utterly different quark.
Our cosmos is a serenade for strings,
And by clicking onto the website we can share
This dance of everything that the Devis do together,
Who are as bright as millions of fires, and moons
Such as Enceladus, the sky's brightest object;
Saturn's dazzling satellite, flexing its mass as it orbits
While its pole's volcanoes blast out ice.

And though we yearn for Andromeda, when we learn
That she's four million light years from our galaxy
While we are less than a mole on Orion's arm,
We see once more that we are merely part of things –
As far from the outer rim of our milk-filled churn
As we are from that galactic bulge at its core.

So let's again take pleasure in the Zodiac cotillion,
The sun partnering each sign in turn,

The dancers stepping together in a way
That demonstrates the combined spiral of a double-helix;
For either the universe has a non-singular origin
Or is neither singular nor many at the start:

A condition then of merging and demerging,
For 'the same aggregate which has been formed in one modification,
Upon a change in the attendant circumstances,
May pass into another: or it may continue
Partaking of the characters of two modifications...'
Unless instead it simply disappears.

Steinhardt and Turok maintain
That we may be living within a membrane
That violently collides every few trillion years
With another nearby. Our cosmos is thus
Attached by strings to a mate. Each is a universe.
Each drives the other's evolution, and the dance

Is an inseparable partnership where all forms are fluid
And ever-changing as the pair keep renewing
Existence after the clash of their culmination;
The one igniting a fire in the other, fluently providing
The hearth to her sparks at a milonga where
Time is the follower, dancing in eternity's embrace.

Heron of Hawthornden

A sequence of dizains for Drue Heinz

*

She fixed her eyes on this yet smiling pond
I would not change for princes' stately courts
My senses one by one gave way to sleep
Lull'd in a slumber by a myrtle shade.
And you her words, words, no, but golden chains,
Delicious, wanton, amiable, fair,
Your joys as ample as their causes are.
What numbers with her enter in this dance
To temper what is moist, dry, hot, and cold?
How sweet are streams to poison drunk in gold.

*

20th November

Our very first breakfast. Tardier than the rest,
I sit alone at the narrow elm table,
Terribly ancient; eating my porridge with Sucrose
Purchased in Tottenham. Not quite as fit
As I ought to be; recovering from a twisted knee,
Everyone else now busily writing. As I finish
What's in my bowl, the elegant dark-wood Windsor
Chair, stately and antique as our patron, who is
A hundred and three, gives way beneath me.
I clutch at its arms, but still... it collapses, albeit gracefully,

Taking me with it, spilling me onto the tartan carpet.
This elicits apology. However, I'm encouraged not to fret.
This veteran's been rickety for ages.
Hamish will fix it. Yes, but the peg at the top of a leg
Splintered, I'm sure, as we keeled over.
Clearly that chair has now been put paid to by me.
What a way to start a residency in a precipitous
Castle, a castle where silence is *de rigeur* until our
Convivial evening fare. I must watch my step
As well as how I sit. There is a dungeon below us here.

21st November

I'm ready to set forth today for the cave of William
Wallace, armed against the cold in my hooded
Wind-cheater worn on top of a padded jacket.
Penny is just coming back. She's given up. The path,
If you can call it that, is just too narrow and treacherous.
Resolute, I persist; slipping off duck-boards into mere
When they're not well-swathed in chicken wire,
Grabbing ineffectual hold of rhododendrons to steady
Myself, helped by the stick she bequeathed me.
Now, through thin and thick, the Wallace prevails.

An ancient beech at a parting of ways, liberally etched,
Implies that this rampart carved from rock secretes
My goal beneath the crag below it. Down the treacherous steps,
I go, to be led along a muddied ledge, into the darkest
Of holes. Can't reach the walls I'm unable to see
But sit inside and sketch: orange of beeches across the ravine,
Yellowing sycamores, firework-bright, through a frame of stone.
Triumphant, I return, sliding most of the way on my bum;
Sweating, soaked too round the back, where I've come
Into contact with mud and loam, moist leaves, moss and bracken.

22nd November

I'm getting into my paint-box, but it's
Far too cold to actually paint in the open. What I do
Is sketch, get in a quick snap or two if I don't forget
My mobile, as I managed to yesterday. At this
Exclusive retreat, I paint in my room from memory.
Goes ok with my view from within that cave,
But now I must work on the sketch from the rampart
Above, gazing away across the drop, a dead tree
In the foreground. Get out the sketch. Look at it, perplexed.
Just a tangle of incomprehensible scratches.

Luckily there's scribbled here and here, *Grey, yellow,*
Orange, grey. Those off-vertical lines must be
The cadaver leaning away, while below is that weird
Green trunk under the crag, reaching horizontally
Over the turbulent Esk. Hours later, I've smeared my attempt
With paint and got nowhere. My greys are too faint;
The orange of my beeches far too red. Looks like Vermont.
This is Scotland for chrissake. Imitating Alex Katz,
I add blown leaves in clumsy snatches. Ruined!
Can I retrieve it? Can I erase that inappropriate leaf?

On day release from the castle now, I take
The 31 from its terminus into town, riding in with Jean,
A Scot, who knows the whole shebang concerning Edinburgh.
A bright, bright morning. Hills a distant brown.
In addition, Jean knows the whole shebang concerning publishing.
Get interns from an MSc. Usually they know their stuff.
Contracts, distribution, promotion, rights, accountancy.
Someone has a seizure. Call an ambulance, quick!
Thank goodness there's a nurse aboard. Let her deal with it.
We all pour out, and rain comes down, heavy, at a slant.

Later, when I decide to head back, the 31 for Polton Mill
Turns up. Do I want it? Where do I reside?
Another 31 pulls in, bound for Bonnyrigg. I board it but
I've got it all mixed up. Am taken deep, deep into
A labyrinthine estate. Waiting to ride back to where the bus-routes
Deviate, I stare out as the driver leafs his paper. Green shelter,
Windows much abused, impossible to see through.
Low wooden barriers set on their diagonals. Grey to beige
Pebble-and-dash, brown rooves, and saplings in stockades.
Each minute passes slower than the one preceding it.

24th November

My sharpener, it's double-barrelled, cherished,
Made of yellow plastic. Pencils of varying sizes find it
Effective. Into the frost I step, neglecting walking boots.
Only going for a stroll along an easy walk that
Leads one under the yews below the crag on which
Our castle perches, then along the river, up and back
Onto the terrace above this ancient seat. I've done the yews
Already. Now I find a spot where, steeply beneath me,
Mixed with a tangle of sodden branches, water the colour of
Tannin whitens between rocks beneath another yew-tree.

Perfect for my purposes! Boldly, I step off the path,
Stand on a rotten stump, sketching away until I drop
My sharpener! Fuck. I crouch to reach it, stretch;
Still can't get my fingers to it, step off the mound,
Slip, slide, slide further, rapidly nearing the murk of
The torrent. Jesus! Bracken, loam and rot afford no brake.
Is this my destiny? Inches from going in, I stop.
Now the question is, How the hell do I get back up?
The slope betrays each foothold, cheats each grip,
And where's my pad and where's my lovely sharpener?

25th November

Again, I step off the bus at the terminus, after
An abject afternoon of failure. Wasted trip into Edinburgh.
I'd gone in, needing to dance, hoping to find a milonga,
Keen to lose the stiffness caused by yesterday's fall.
Ah, but that vaunted tango 'brunch' only happens once
A month, and not on this particular Saturday. So I am told by
My laptop in a café which offers WiFi – not to be had at
Our remote chateau. I've told the staff I won't be back
For supper. What shall I do? Buy an external player and
Some headphones maybe, maybe snacks to nibble later.

Thus, at the darkening end of day, I step off
At the terminus, loaded down with Bresaola slices,
Rolls, a Lidl chunk of pizza, laptop, headphones,
Player, tango shoes etcetera. Stagger up the road
Towards the distant castle gates, and the distance
Seems to stretch and stretch in front of me, but what
A magnificent sunset! Seen through a line of trees.
Long streaks of vibrant crimson, streaks in line
With the height of distant hills, trees like spidery sentinels;
The sky aglow behind each silhouette.

26th November

Towering above its crag, the castle dominates
This chasm, posing grandly for my pencil through a
Tangle of divested branches. Holly dangles
Gemlike berries. Rhododendrons ever freshly green
Spring up near my feet. A foot to the left, the edge,
And a precipice sheer to the Esk inducing vertigo.
One circular turret rises up above the vertical rock,
Topped by a conical hat. The stone is of a pinkish hue.
Here within these walls, William Drummond of
Hawthornden sat correcting his sonnets and his madrigals.

'Alexis, here she stayed, among these pines'
We wander under, so he tells us, evergreen amidst
Mightily moulting beeches. Here he strolled, I guess,
Gossiping with courtly Ben, who had walked from London
To converse with him. Here I sketch and paint
As Autumn turns to Winter. What might it have been
Like to be pressed, poisoned with hemlock, hung,
Drawn and quartered, or to saunter off
To Flanders as a mercenary? Violently uncertain were their times,
And yet they wrote such deeply loving poetry.

27th November

Artificial coals grow bright above the glowing bars
Installed in the drawing-room fireplace. Here,
We gather after supper. One of us falls back
Onto a couch, the others opt for sofas and armchairs.
Would you prefer to be supposed evil or stupid?
What would you write just for commercial gain?
And is there a vice that leaves you distinctly untempted?
Which animal's hindlegs would you pick out for your own?
We're just a handful of writers, digesting our work and our chow.
Silent all day, our conversation may not come easily now.

Silence reasserts itself, then fresh observation or query
May provoke laughter. Poets and novelists, non-fiction pundits:
Favourite topics are poetry, publishing, presidents, paedophilia.
How many thousands did *you* get today? Busy with his
Water-colours, Wallace feels contrite. When it's what's expected
Of him, how the hell can he write? Nevertheless, one might
Add corrections to what one has come to regard as an
Opus, add a couple more to this sequence of dizains,
And there's been research as to which is the smokiest whiskey,
While one of our novelists climaxed. We're doing alright.

28th November

Chandeliers, unlit, but cast in silhouette
Onto the wall by spots. Below them turn the dancers.
Each couple must negotiate the world of their embrace
While avoiding other worlds. I bussed into the city
Earlier than attendance at this tango night required.
Managed to get to a charity shop secreting
Esoteric CDs. Dined on squid in a hot chilli sauce
Served me by Malays. Now I'm retrieving my breath,
Clad in my esoteric pinstripe-effect pyjamas
Purchased from Primark, perfect for when I connect.

Pleased to be here, finally having completed
My draft of *The Step is the Foot* before my basket arrived.
Well, I'm forever announcing I'm done; finished, finished
So quick, eager as any young puppy might be
To bring you his favourite stick, until some additional shit –
Insight, observation or item just let drop in conversation
Prompts me to include, adjust; infuriating editors.
Is anything ever completed? I dance with Konstantina,
A voluptuous twenty-something. She is an excellent partner.
And this will certainly not be our ultimate tanda.

The wicker picnic basket appears outside my door.
I'm so immersed, I fail to get up from whatever it is
Engages me. The basket sits there for an hour.
Still, the soup keeps warm within its silver thermos.
The sandwiches stay fresh, carefully swathed in clingfilm.
No one ever filches my banana. Each of us gets
Their individual basket. Nothing at all is permitted
To interfere with our practice. This stately place is
Made of hush, a hush that must envelop us –
As in the palace of the Beast, Beauty was a solitary

Attended hand and foot by deft but invisible servants.
Of its own accord, the flagon tipped to fill her cup,
Which floated gently towards her, while the curtains
Drew themselves, just as her bath chose to rise
From the bottom up and tapers lit the candles there,
Held in no one's hands. A sponge moved ever so gently
Over her blemishless back. She stepped out into a towel,
Otherwise alone, as each is here, even if a housekeeper
May moan if we neglect to bring our baskets back to her
Before the last dregs of the soup have congealed in our thermoses.

30th November

Ben's bricklayer's hands were matter for mockery.
I can imagine him crushing the palm of our
Aristocratic laird, whose cosmopolitan mitts
Fitted as smoothly as Scotch into his Florentine gloves.
Had he expected 'courtly' Ben to be a mite more courtly
Than his Plebeian origins allowed? Nails were pulled
And fingers lopped. Jacobean history abounds in unsavoury
Mention of hands. None could be filthier, it is recorded,
Than those of their monarch: left forever unwashed
In case a decent scrub should affect their sensitivity.

Lovelace loved to snog his chaste Lucasta's gloves.
My own hands toy with my beard – habit that infuriates me.
Think of the thousand and one fair hands
That must have scribbled here. Mine open Drummond's book
At his *Tears on the Death of Moeliades*.
'In Cypress sad, glad Hymen's torches change.'
Strange his wife-to-be should heavenward ascend
The very day they'd chosen to be bound in wedlock:
Precious hand entwined with precious hand.
It sent him far from Hawthornden, self-exiled, overseas.

'She set her by these musked eglantines...'
I'd love some for my garden. They'd be cherished.
Ah, but what's an eglantine? Can you pick them up
In a garden centre? 'Eglantines, Sir? No,
We don't appear to stock them. You could try B&Q.'
Casting for the scent, I climb the lichened steps
That lead one to the library in the walled orchard
Summiting the knoll above this castle and its chasm;
Slip through the greenhouse into the quiet modernity
Of rooms containing artbooks, fiction, back-issues and poetry,

As well as landscape gardening's coffee-table slabs.
No help at all. Perhaps below, where reference books
Are kept. So later I unlatch the iron-studded door
At the foot of our sturdy keep. Inside, I find
The *RSNC Guide* and *The Oxford Book of Wild Flowers.*
Neither of these worthies boasts an eglantine,
And I am in despair. Only *Collins' Dictionary* rewards
With, 'Same as sweetbriar!' Yes! 'On chalky soil...'
I know it from the downs, when I rode my pony there.
However, *Oxford* qualifies its provenance, 'In Scotland, rare.'

This is a bookish citadel. The roofs are tiled
With books. Tomes comprise the steps. Hereditary
Portraits are replaced by Gore Vidal, Huxley and Cocteau –
(Not very good ones, it has to be said – proportions all askew
– Visual art's subservient here to the vice of literature).
I'm deep in Jean's biography of her great-great-uncle
Scott Moncrieff – whose English *Temps Perdu* is reckoned
An improvement. Earlier, some fairly mundane view
Was aired about the seduction of the young. 'C.K.'
Was a slim ephebe wooed by the set admiring Wilde.

That was back when being gay could see you locked
Away for several months in Wormwood Scrubs.
No one could tell *me* who I should or should not fuck
When I was growing up. Later I taught writing to
The 'vulnerable' in the Scrubs. Sex offenders, upper-crust
Bounders, nonces and bent cops. Kept apart from
The crooks. The poor do over your property,
The rich do over your kids. These days, being correct
Demands we frown on vicious, underage desires,
But C.K. was maimed by the war, not by his older admirers.

3rd December

Even the cook has written a book! Her *Scottish Country*
Cooking must be a must for the staff (or wife) of any laird
Hosting an ambitious shoot. The book is stuffed
With recipes that stimulate the imagination as they do
The palate: Joy's warm asparagus, pear and
Parma ham salad, Lamb with a garlic, chestnut
And tomato relish, White chocolate mousse
With nectarine and raspberry coulis, and homemade
Ginger ice that leaves the wraith of its flavour
In the mouth after the last glob has been consumed.

A game specialist, there's nothing wraithlike about Ruth,
Clad in her Dalmatian bottoms, good for getting
Down in when she checks her oven. Dinner is served
On Sunday nights in the formal dining-room
With its large round table graced by tall Corinthian
Candlesticks, and on the sideboard Ruth announces here for us
Her fresh salmon and dill filo parcels begirt
By a Hollandaise sauce, served between one of her
Scrumptious hors d'oeuvres and a most original dessert.
Can Hamish get the keeper to provide her with a deer for us?

4th December

Deer and a shoot seem to satisfy everyone.
There is a general desire to devour a haunch
Of venison. But breakfast is becoming tense.
It's my fault. Haven't the sense to keep
My mouth shut. Cultural ladies and gents
Like nothing better than to bathe together in agreement's
Glow. Eagerly, this issue scrubs the back of that.
Empathy, and just how *much* you care about
Suits everyone but Wallace though. A huntsman blooded
These cheeks. I shall defend the badge this represents.

My son and I sat watching the fight from the *ombra*.
There was a powerful pride, the pride of beasthood,
In the bull there bloodied, black, and sinking to his knees.
Why should this deny me my right to be a socialist?
Leave empathy to dear old Lady Bountiful.
Let clever girls get on with their careers
Instead of marrying rather well and sponsoring
Some dear old cottage hospital. Bring on,
Bring on the Welfare State! Leave me the right to holloah,
Hunt to hounds and clear the five-bar gate.

5th December

One of the very last leaves floats towards
The warbling Esk, as a butterfly might flutter here
At the height of summer. Winter's not all
Misery. I'm seated on some rudimentary bench
Carved directly out of the crag. Moss upholsters
Its gouged stone which overlooks the stream's
Turn. Winter removes her clothes for me;
Anorexic perhaps; however, there is a loveliness
To her bones. We see more everyday
Of the sleekly descending pennons of the pines.

And now I know where I am. I am where
She stayed. I am sitting within *his* frame
As the winter ushers her downstream in some
Physical way, just as all of us must go,
And yet in some poetic sense she's never left
This perfect realm. Chanced upon, years later,
Didn't Drummond's second lady look exactly like her,
Just as a floating leaf looks like a butterfly?
As I rise, a heron lifts from below me...
Floats upstream, and can I help but be certain it is he?

6th December

The Ladyboys of Bangkok are playing Bonnyrigg
Or somewhere very like it. Can't quite read the poster
Now cabin fever takes me into Edinburgh.
Windows offer kilts and sporrans, Harris Tweed
And Shetland jumpers, yes, but nowhere's quite
As typical as one thinks it ought to be. Zenobia,
Palmyra's queen, watches closely from the falafel house
Across the street. Heritage is now a trademark.
Shrunken bagpipes or a tartan dog-coat might
Be better than that mini-kilt with imitation straps.

Fairy-lights are everywhere, wound about pine bunting.
Outside every chapel, banners say, Try Praying.
Father Christmas waves the punters into his free parking lot
Down the road where sawn-off trees are sold.
Penny got lost in a maze of these in the Christmas market.
She tried praying and found a way out. Later
She witnessed Father Christmas being aggressively piped
Into Stockbridge, drawn by a team of living reindeer.
Easy to wilt in a sporran, since Jean suggests you keep
Coinage in it, should you get a hard-on in your kilt.

7th December

All day I have kept to my room, engaged in writing
Or reading, as the wind went wolfishly between
The roofs, the chimneys and the walls, wrapping lean
Flanks around our single turret and the keep.
Overhanging a sheer drop, my room is a captain's cabin
Looking down on the wake from the tall poop
Of a galleon. Yew boughs are the deep, swirling below,
While, across the rival swell of the ravine, a fleet
Of spars goes careering wherever I'm taken,
Driven by this raging gale into far flung memories

Or into wry thoughts of this secluded castle's prime;
Reading how, as Jonson gossiped, Drummond wrote it down.
Queen Elizabeth, the courtier swore, was a virgin
Purely on account of an unbreachable membrane.
The queen was quite reciprocal, with gentlemen,
But too afraid to let a surgeon take his lancet to her cunt,
Even though a brace of heads of state were keen
To penetrate *that* citadel. Never would she pose
Before a loyal mirror in old age, and so it was that those
Who painted her would sometimes put vermilion on her nose.

8th December

We scribblers seem to have reached the scrape-the-barrel
Stage, while Richard de Marco is probably gilding
The lily. Every poster, flyer, letter, sketch or squib
Is kept in the archive of his instigations, which he shows
Me now while taking snapshots of me being so shown.
Ricky is a Scottish squirrel, hoarding the art he has
Brought to the 'New Jerusalem' from far flung ends
Of Europe: Serb and Bosnian, Pole, Rumanian – famous
Names, obscurities. Kantor draws for him a line
Of 'Demarcation' – corporate alienation versus the imagination.

Back in the castle's drawing-room, Rob, our zoological
Authority whose book is *Moles*, shows us how he
Can make a wedge between his fingers which is genetic,
Possibly, though I maintain you can train for it. Jean
Can wriggle her ears, Penny undulate her throat
As if she were a turtle. Diffidently, I demonstrate
How I have taught myself to purr on the inhale
As well as the exhale; and then Phil whose poems
Reach to the interstices of what others write about
Goes into the attributes of his cats in considerable detail.

9th December

Nothing about this castle seems haunted to me.
About the Esk, I'm not so sure. Penny and I set out
In boots and mountain wear to walk the far side
Of the ravine. The map misread, we start from the wrong
Bridge along a disused railway line, trudge past
Tracts of meadow glazed with frost, finally reach the
Path, to find ourselves down by the bank, then on the ridge
Looking down; the frozen state of muddied ground
A boon. We trace the writhings of this peat-stained artery,
Scrambling upstream, to enter haunted territory.

The torrent bursts into cascades below moments
Of pure vertigo. Pink stone or grey. Heights looked out
Across at now unveil their secret fissures. Dark
Ravine between castles that have dealt with sieges.
Climbing towards the source, we come across antiquity.
Here some god of the wood may change you into a tree.
Penny turns into Penelope. Three agile roe deer thread
Their way directly up to the high ground after a drink.
Poetry has shared these views since the sun first sank.
And there is our castle, tall on the opposite bank.

'Ornate' is not ornate enough a word
For barley twist pillars and beasts that bend around
Pilasters much as the roe deer bend around crags
In the near ravine. Sunlight pours through haloes.
Leaded branches allow for illumination of oakleaves.
Greedy vines come sprouting out of a green man's mouth.
The devil proposes a threesome. Dangling boughs
Of stone overhang old ladies in enormous camel overcoats.
This is a chapel in dreadlocks. Plaited Curly kale
Spirals sculpted beams in Dionysiac revelry.

Only vacant ledges point to Puritan objection.
Merlin is interred here in a set he shares with a badger
Under the crypt. Hairy angels give me such an uplift!
A black cat actually parades between the pews
To sniff the Second Advent candle as it's being lit.
Now the priest bemoans 'Winterval' – idiot word
Adopted by Birmingham Council. Yes, a thousand years are
But a day. Candles vie with the sun to set bouquets afire.
Elements dissolve and the dead become the quick.
The kilted gent with a dirk up his sock wears a jewel in his ear.

Each Northern night I dance in the Masque of Blackness,
Make to revere Queen Ann of Denmark and attendant ladies.
Darkly they dance, their skirts in flounces drawn by
Inigo Jones. They dance bare-breasted, to enthral;
Indifferent to the symbolism intended, much to Ben's
Disgust, their ivory made ebony. I twirl
With La Gialletta Gallante, sun-burned, exotic
Beauty celebrated by Cherbury, who lauded all things
Black. Poop and prow, my castle galleon dances
On the night, and then I'm taken under, into its depths.

The deep overwhelms all contours. I feel I'm dark
Internally, at one with night's material. Seeing without sight,
I burrow through my sleep, or patrol its tunnels now,
Pouncing on dreams to consume as the mole bites into
Her worms when she comes across them. All too often, though,
My sleep is shallow in the wee small hours. Barely beneath
The turf, it's all too easy to surface; ancient bladder
Prompting me to pee, and then it's breakfast time.
Unwilling to concede, the Scottish night just pastes itself
More firmly to the panes as I switch on the light.

12th December

Sucrose, Splenda and a sprinklable powder
Which goes by the name of Xylotol provide me
With alternatives that compensate for the sweetness
Of a tooth; one of the teeth, it has to be,
Which remain to me. Alcohol depletes my energy,
So I permit myself a tot only after an interval
Of several days. I try to maintain a regime
Of physical jerks. Happily, my knees
Are bearing up beneath me at last, good
For walks across fields with an icing of frost.

Jean believes I have had my way with a jaguar,
When I only said how very nice they were,
Referring to the car; and in a self-deprecatory
Mood tonight, Wallace happens to relate
How he hit upon his favourite dating site. Well,
He had detected that, while hardly affluent,
Being somewhat older, even being a lot,
Was tolerable to a third of the women using it
To secure themselves a partner. 'Splenda
Daddy!' Penny quips. The castle rocks with laughter.

13th December

So, if a castle should have hidden an unconscious
It would be located beneath its furnished rooms.
Hamish now unlocks a lowly door, takes us under
The keep into caverns hollowed out of the sandstone
Which has already yielded chimneys, precipices, coombs
Sculpted by the industrious stream racing through
This canyon of its own making. Grottoes gouged by chisel,
Colder than our own accommodation, possibly
Billeted troops or stored provision. This one leads
To a doocot underground with apertures to crags:

Home to doves with a castle floating on their wings.
Elsewhere, under iron lid, a dungeon one could be
Lowered into; lavatory of stone suggesting that your
Stay could last a while. Have I a subterranean extension,
Well of desires, dungeon for thoughts which need
Some rudimentary place to shit? Have I a doocot
Brooding flights repressed which give me the slip
In slips of the tongue, or uncompleted business
Stored in hyperthermic neglect; a grief, I guess,
Locked off in one nether chamber hardly even mentioned?

Did Coleridge score his opium off De Quincy?
Would that he had! A legend might be made.
Who would have thought De Quincy lived at Lasswade?
A mere stone's throw away. Please allow this perfectly
Romantic take. It is a nice idea. Perhaps
They shared a vision via ESP – that
Would make the Esk the Alph, and this
Its 'cedern chasm'. Now we have the sacred river
Running through the caverns, in the sense of *past*,
Down to the sea at Leith, sunless for most of the year.

Rosslyn, further up, has its chapel that could euphuistically
Be called a stately pleasure dome. And maybe
The person from Porlock took a leaf from Jonson's book,
Interrupting Coleridge on his residency.
Me, I'd love to plant the potent poppy in some
Sheltered corner of the walled orchard,
Or at least a poke of marijuana seeds
Purchased from the head shop could be scattered there
To roll up when in bloom in the petals of the eglantine.
Now that would make a pretty lucent pillar.

15th December

He put her off, perhaps, with too much verse,
Since first he caught her skinny dipping with
Her two companions in the Ore. River across
The Firth from here. We walk beyond a copse
Of silver birch, through the musky odours of the deer
Who leave their imprint in the ferns, as she
Left hers, after she finally paid him that visit,
Off the track, downstream, where a spit
Twists the Esk round an islet. Drummond sonneteers
Her eyes of green while I imagine a bath-house.

Rudimentary sauna, sunk in these ruined walls
Sheltered by yews and a myrtle bush from prying eyes.
'The graces naked danc'd about the place.'
Could it have been a bath-house? I ask Hamish,
Who hasn't a clue, but says, *à propos* of that
Sandy beach, perfect for swimming and sunning,
Just past the islet, where the shallows loiter now in winter light,
That running once he chanced upon two naked women
Bathing there, who waved at him and smiled – but
Where was the third? He didn't stop because he was running.

Hawthornden, 2017

Empyrean Suite

POEMS FROM THE AFTERLIFE

By Fawzi Karim – in my versions

I can see everything from the sky:
An everything that's rather far away.
They are having quite a struggle lowering the box
I am not in any more into its hole.
It's true, I did not want to go, and now
One of the grave-digger's planks has fallen
       and got in the way of the soil they are shovelling in.
All rather embarrassing. Anthony looks up,
Admires the clouds which are special today: even I
       can see that, from this, my privileged vantage-point.
They're as various as clouds can ever be, cirrus wisps
       as well as flotillas of cumulus.
Gwendolyn is discussing nomads with a man
       who has just returned from Iran.
She mentions Mesopotamian tablets which describe
       how the nomads several thousand years ago
       were much the same as they are now;
Useful when their herds dunged the land,
       but when the first shoots came
       the farmers had to pay them to move on.
I feel I've been moved on before my time
Which the white-capped dignitary, obligatory
       at such occasions, seeks by his prayers to delay,

As Lily remarks, wishing that he'd get a move on
in a loud, unarabic voice.
But Samer reads out his favourite poem of mine,
and I can see that Anthony is pleased
– even a tear in his eye.

§

I seat myself in the cockpit of a spitfire,
  looking out of this photograph from the war
  on the wall of the Greenwood Hotel.
It is thus I observe my wake.
Which is being held in the backroom that's been booked,
Where in the Blitz, officers of the RAF would gather with their
  Scotch and sodas,
Keeping an eye on the young ones dancing next door in the ballroom.
Surveillance as discreet as is my own.
My sons are smoking at the benches outdoors,
  distanced from the Arabic inside,
  where even Anthony recalls the *Gardenia,*
  although he was never there.
Through all our exiled years,
  we've held reunions here, in this room;
Our discussions as intense as in that bar back in Baghdad,
Back in the bad old days that now look good.
Each poet rises to proclaim a eulogy.
Anthony notes how Semitic most of us look.
Big noses and bald heads, just like his Jewish uncles.
Now the dark wine turns to blood
  as everyone drinks back
  into the past of the Middle East.
We wonder what it's all about – from Northolt.

§

Since Anthony must be my medium now,
Rendering these afterthoughts in yet more of his versions,
Having done two books of mine already,
I will help him enter in realms
        that I've been given access to, in this, my disembodied state.
I've met his daughter Storm, in his dream:
He's trying to put her together as if she were Lego.
The pieces are so small, he does it clumsily.
For an artist, clumsiness is a sin.
He stares down at his hands.
Is she so small because of the distance of years?
The sentences in dreams may not make sense,
        and yet a dream may sentence you – to grief?
Were I alive, at this juncture,
        we'd discuss the way
        meaning alters as speech changes its part.
The word is seldom fixed,
        any more than the swimmer
        can stay in one place in the Tigris,
Except, that is, in a picture.

§

Yesterday, I went boating with my father.
Lily seems to get on better with me as a memory, I told him.
He made no reply, busied himself with an oar,
      pushed us off a cloud into the azure.
We have to watch out for drones, he told me,
And vapour trails and Boeings and bullshit and false flags.
I asked him what we were fishing for.
How should I know? he replied.
You never quite get used to this state of non-being.
It's too abstract, nothing you can get your teeth into.
The bottom of our river was the Earth.
But as we fished, the depths appeared to get deeper.

Are we fishing for thoughts of us from below, I wondered,
      before accepting that our lines no longer reached that far.

§

Basil sat by my grave today,
      reading me my poems.
I must say it was difficult to hear,
Being far above, rather than below and near.
He then began to write himself.
      I'm not sure what I felt.
Should I be apprehensive? Should I be pleased?

A goodbye nonetheless...
Felt by the wind's breeze,

The earth's opening and the closure
Shared between the minds of mere mortals.

Let the soil welcome our hero . . .
Did the poem need both wind and breeze?
I tried hard not to be critical.
The sun beams down,
Draining the dirt of any moisture . . .
That I liked: it was accurate.
It had been hard to break the clods with a shovel
     on the day of my funeral.
If only I could have shown him by a gesture
     that I was there, if not quite at his shoulder.

Like a lost moral-less thief seeking a compass
     to guide him . . .
Basil standing lost, seeking serenity.

But all of us are lost, it seems to me.
And he should remind himself
     that something of me is inside him.

§

It is advisable to attain detachment.
So the sages tell us. This is why
They seek the highest shelters to practise immobility
Above the summer pastures of the goats.
Not that this is new to me.
I've practised it before, learning to adapt
        to relinquishing Baghdad,
Leaving all behind me: the stamping ground of Gilgamesh,
        the watering-holes, oases of good wine
        and fiery conversation.
Enchanted stretches of river, our boat, our mulberry tree, my father.
Now I'm obliged to leave behind
        aspects of a newer life I was still getting accustomed to.
The end, for instance, of exile:
Learning to resist its title foisted on my verse.
Anthony would scold me when I voiced the faintest nostalgia.
You're just as much a part of London's literary life
        as I am now. And it was true. And yet, in death,
I must surrender to life my British sons, my Greenford home,
        my culinary contests with my brother.
It seems I am obliged to go into exile again.
Here, I will have to address myself
        to coming to terms with heavenly renditions
        of unearthly symphonies,
Giving up all my CDs
And bidding adieu to the Central Line.

§

The gentlest sprinkle of rain
    as dawn lightens gaps between curtains
    in the bedrooms of my loved ones.
Perhaps you will think of me, my darlings,
    Every time you find yourselves awake
    in the summer, just before the break
Of daylight, before the business of being alive
    must begin again, as begin it must.
If you toss and turn, think of how I am done with that,
Done at last with the body
    and all the discomfort it's been causing me.
Let us be thankful for small mercies.
This is what they say, the Brits – a phrase at which
    I've scratched my head.
But now let it work as a balm
    on all disquiet, bring with it calm.
Let us be thankful for small mercies.
Let us be thankful for small mercies.
Let us be thankful for small mercies.

§

And now my thoughts grow fainter
        in the inner ear of my interpreter.
Up here, I've been asking for ink.
I am told that it's a commodity
        no one sees a reason to provide
Given our immortal immateriality.
        Pen and paper prove as rare indeed.
There is a perfectly decent bar
        since it's quite acceptable to drink.
Here, I've been chatting with Abu Nawaz
        with Rumi and Li Po.
Sappho is here as well, and drinking rather heavily
        with Emily Dickinson, who hardly
        touched a drop below.
Here there's no discrimination, and a wine
        of such excellent vintage we refer to it as an elixir.
Dante suggests I dip my nib
        into the night – I haven't a nib.
He tried it once with his finger but gave up.
Less and less did I feel the need to say anything anymore.
Instead, for centuries, he's traced
        letters he discovers by linking star to star.
Not much of what he gets from this makes sense,
        but Ashbery approves of the results.

Envelopes

Mark Lombardi, 1961–2000. American neo-conceptual artist who
specialized in drawings that document alleged financial and political
frauds by power brokers, government agencies and organised crime,
thus mapping abuses of control. His suicide by hanging is disputed.

To push the envelope derives from early supersonic use,
Referring to constraints you don't exceed with safety.
Ask of Mark Lombardi where was his off-ramp.
A bail-out by his Texan heiress? Elegance gone lefty.
From a censored 'other side', warblers in camouflage,
Witch birds or ghost birds, hid within their habitats,
Tweet or leak less popular interpretations of our acts;
But watch for those East Europe gals: Nazi-types but tasty.

Cold war. Soft war. Fat war. Thin war
Tic-toked from the Emirates' city-dangling cable-car,
That counter-offensive proves largely a mirage.
But who around here disputes the force-fed optics?
Keen to push *their* envelope, unelected leaders rant
About how, if their team loses to a phrase initially
Limited to space flight, it will be harder to argue
For democracy as a sound system of government.

But that's the venture thrill of firepower sponsorship.
Viz. to surpass normal limits and bring off a bet
Viewed as radical or risky. Capital, Progress and War.
And miracles by Jesus, each with arms attached to it,
As quips Larry Johnson when another sortie leads to sure
Obliteration, brushing matters back to the false

Cross of propaganda dreamt up by the Vatican.
Fatalities increased by their anti-retreat force

Weighed against the lure of mission creep.
Envelope is such a pregnant word. Our Jingoists keep
Pushing theirs – should it burst all hell breaks out –
And what you sow as surely shall ye reap.
Was Lombardi pushing his after its initial usage
Spread to each edgy pursuit, finally to find its way
Into his boundary-shift activity? Item how Duchamp
Pushed it with a urinal, back in the modernists' day.

Five eyes crown our intelligence machine.
Where does machinery end, intelligence begin?
In some *Haut de la Garenne* where the Clodes meet Gwythian Prins...
Backers of black ops, marketeers of hypersonic luxury;
A leader's limousine developed by the same
Group as makes his battle tanks. Or think Rolls-Royce
Or some wonder weapon touted, with its fancy tote-bag:
Pounder fit for Belgorad, or where they shape the battlefield,

Reducing the brigades, hunting down each target, wall by
Blessed wall. Those five eyes. We know their code word
Is *Versailles*. Zoroaster cognates Friesian antecedents
Ever since the great flood. Armament demands a Spartan policy.
But armament is an appealing, power-indulging industry.
Hephaistos found the time to weave that sumptuous net of gold
In which he caught his wife with Aries. Envelope
That fitted snug. Perhaps his wife was in on it...

Whereas Kashoggi Junior needed to be hacked to bits
In order to be fitted into his. Graft seduces hope and fear,
Making it a threesome, as he told *Der Speigel*.
Let us all jerk off to our 'copters circling the turf
And banish from our minds the collapse of what
Took things away, the noble sewage disposal conduit
Perfect for our mop-up corps – as directed by the first
Post-Modern PM; not, as dictatorial types may go,

Much of a player in this affair, unlike the vulnerable Beard.
Again, it's the optics, stupid. That and gold and London Brent.
We're not equipped, we've not the *Stik*, so to speak,
To counter those thermobarbaric – no, Joe, get it right.
Thermobaric rockets. Looks like combat has moved on
Since Sir Philip Sidney's time. Consummate courtier, yes,
But no Nelson, his was a flashy and unnecessary death,
Only one year shy of the Tudors-under-thirty club.

It takes twenty-one defensive darts to halt a single Zircon
In its tracks. Forget fresh air. Grieve for the shadow
Before you, muddled by the shadows of leaves and the breeze
Which is beyond the launch capabilities of the Aegus Ships
Serving as escorts – flouncing over some ocean to the East
In the Navy's most dramatic bellicose formation.
Yes, it's the Carrier Battle Group. Walk away from the war,
And you become fixated on the problems of your own career.

There is the reality of conflict. There is a contest of illusions
For your soul. And there is doom porn to deal with and
The journo who says it's other journos use the boot on him the most.
It's like the poets diss your zone for all the dulcet use of tone:
The taciturn, derelict hinterland of a spider town
On a web it has spun that it would take more than a few
Thermobarics to obliterate, our post-modern cox
Asserts reassuringly. Ah, but the Rohingya face abyss.

The Sunnis loathe the Shia since Asunder Land's
The object since Korea. Rejecting all divergence from *their* plan,
By secret ballot blackballing the RAND, our deep ones carry on
Marketing aggressive kit – rewarded, and informed.
So for a spell it's best that you forgo the here and now.
It's not as if you haven't paid a visit there before
And found yourself again in the same frustrating pit,
Which is a bore, and yet, beware. In the 'way back when'

And in your imaginary 'after', interest enslaves you and supports
Spyware while many of your worst nightmares have been or
Are being realised somewhere. Maybe in Sutton Coldfield or
In Severodanask. Sure, there are bougies in tower-block enclaves,
But they're just lambs to the slaughter authorised by the hawks
At the Brookings Institute, according to Bloomberg;
They're buying off cartels with a price-crime pipe-lining Asia
At an all-time high as Bobby Azarian cuts down on his shower-time.

Here, the glaring issue isn't speed, so weigh up the attractors,
Plus the fictive states of stability. You can pre-order your javelin
At GM's man-portable systems or try the Fire-and-Forget
Anti-tank missile any girl can guide towards her rival.
It was designed to defeat heavily-armoured peccadilloes,
With Aphrodite leaning from the cockpit of her turret
While lighter-skinned military come rolling in her wake
Along with her stylist, her publicist, her soda-jerk.

We go in with whatever we can field. Just dismiss our losses as
A visual Tinnitus irritating screens. They brush off
The weapon which also has capability against other cups of tea,
Taboo except when searched for on the dark.
Boudoirs, barracks, combat detox centres, not to mention
Bunkers and bolt-holes, all for thirty-thousand USD,
And no questions asked of the dark, as snug beneath official domes
We're busy taking upskirts of human calculators

Chalking up the numbers they're assiduously crunching
On the catwalks raised to reach enormous survey boards
In some vintage conflict. Beauty a *vivandière*
Before Joan of Arc raised the *fleur-de-lys* as standard.
Now she projects her hologram onto the night, as the stenographic
Crew for the Western Empire seeks to avoid all interlocks
And connections, interdicting link analysis, meta-data;
Shooting off both feet instead, then seeking to impose

Restrictions as to where to tread among the gong farmers
Ratteners and gaudy dancers with no cognisance of anything this deep.
Hollywood plots have their cake and eat it days,
As is the case with coverage of Tom Cruise in Wonderland
Aiming at some looking-glass with a lack of parity
In netcentric warfare. Should you meet a stinger, use a dock.
No thirty-million package of Burkean conservatism's
Gonna wrest control back from the Wing.

What links data to skirmish experience is a paradigm on leverage
For informational dominance over glory hounds
But words can go no further at this point. Self-interest
And ignorance overwhelm the portals. Riot bucks authority.
And so you look after your base, as did Merrick Garland
In the Oklahoma cover-up. No armchair warlord
Can be adamant he's batting for consensus
While at work embezzling an unsuspecting treasury –

Or is it in cahoots – like the Mafia, cathedrals and freemasonry?
For one assumes a face behind the fencing-mask
Or is that simply a figment? Still, it would seem the done thing.
Men are always eager for attack, at least they say they are.
Their weapons sexed by nicknames: Ass-to-Mouth, Uncle's Teen –
You get to know a fellow by his categories: PMC and POV.
She twerks into ground-based position. Shaping the battlefield
Saucily now. Bitchy Aphrodite of Apocalypse:

Hers is the jargon of chess and l'épée, assuming
Symmetrical conflict, which it never is. Riposte, feint, lunge...
Castle, move your knight again. Boycott the referendum.
Identify the axis of resistance and destroy.
Bombs or boobs? You ask any family. Everyone invites
You to invest in their own issue of weaponry.
Look at the pride a gangster takes in his moll,
Though beneath synthetic grass, dust replaces soil.

His family maintain that Mark was a hellion as well as a
Chronic envelope-pusher, pushing his way into art,
Making it his bag, his own concept – distillation
Interlock by interlock of crooked realms, metastasizing
Money illegitimately hot into money innocently
Hot for an investment; making use of one honed
Anti-Trust accounting tool to portray entire spheres of influence
Much as how Mantegna paints a coven of Gonzagas.

Our Defense Unicorns have subsidized the escalation;
Suits their centaur temperaments to turn the heat up, Forbes reports,
Burning us all in one breath. Opportune that Stockholm Syndrome
Even affects the cannibal's victim, who begs to be eaten of course.
No mosaic corpses in Uganda: no mosaic nookie on ex-hamster.
Get them onside, those firebrand clerics we blame,
Funding them thru Shield AI or thru Rebellion Defense.
Market hostility, give it good looks. Use a mix explosive and intense.

The Photographer

But what surface is smoother than the slow slope
Of a beach at night, carpeted by shawls of surf
In a darkness overlaid by lace fringes and palm trees?
As she shook her mane at you, you'd shoot her suit beside a sea
Measured in its toppling, exercising with due gravitas.

That was back in the sixties, jobbing for Harpers & Queen,
And the work had its perks. There was a dark room.
Buddies in the avant-garde had negs they'd scratch and stain,
But you were more into rock stars, cocktail shoots on location.
Later on, instead of models, you had students within reach.

All that was then, and you give up, having moved your parasol,
And not being able to get it sunk so deep into the beach
As the hooded woman who rents them out at a discount,
It is now embarrassing its lodger by keeling over
Again and again, spurred on by an almost laughing breeze

While overdoing its trick obeisance for the sake
Of sugarcane or banana. Glad to get some work for once,
Shooting sights as destinations, sifting through your images:
A spread for Thailand tours in an inflight magazine –
Not much cash but easy enough since you retired here

Ages ago, if at a loss now, as you get more rickety
Without the language. Do not ask the Brahmins, partner.
Even Home-Pro has its spirit house. For relief you worship
Sinks and lavatories, understand your pooh is full of auguries.
The sun can't help but cast its glitter over dated blades,

Improving what's distilled in their alembic. Pairs immobile in the sea.
At a stalemate, out of sorts, discomforted by lemurs.
Torrential rains have fallen for perhaps a hundred thousand years,
Losing the gist of whatever Spring was meant to be.
You wanted all your students to appreciate the moon,

For the 'seasonal purpose' of the plough is to turn
Over the upper layer of soil, bringing fresh nutrients
To the top, while burying husks, the cinders after the reap
And both weed and yield seeds, obliging these to snap
And so provide a seed-free basis for a different crop.

Flip the image, crop it, stop. Try weaving with the lens
Or think of the eye as a plough. Blades curve after each other.
The monkey-pod blooms into shape. It's greenery becomes a hill
From afar. Underneath it's a filagree beginning at the tips
Of twigs that give its crab-like shell its own leafy backdrop.

Consort of an almost equally ancient dowager who has you
Ferried from attraction to attraction, fixing what unloads
To paste it into those free brochures one picks up off the sand
Blown from the tour guide's beach bar stand,
You realise now that you are no more than a conduit,

More puzzled here today than when you first began to try
To apprehend its enigmas, peering out of the taxi
To shoot the mighty pinnacles as they hurtled by
Leering over the ring-road, housing affluent millions
Looking down on parterre projects in their nest of slip-roads.

Used to be the Siamese pitched their tents and pavilions
Wherever they chanced to wind up for the night
Set alight by their own gold. They'd take these flimsy
Structures down when moving on, following the tigers.
Buildings that have overcome the sky itself

Now pitch up behind her grandfather's house.
Buildings dependent on poles 10,000 times
More durable than diamonds get fitted together like tents
That generate quite astronomical rents.
Here is an infinity of storeys. Meanwhile yesterday's block

Gets besooted, the day before's balconies collapse,
And Grandfather's library, drilled by single-pixel worms,
Carries another Pound ABC, this one less popular now
Than it was in its day. Economics, and, as you recall,
A denunciation of all things usuary, paying for cash as wrong

As eating people. Meanwhile *Hitler, Whence and Whither*,
Winds up next to *How to be an Alien*. A newspaper man,
Who saw the world from several points of view,
I am a Camera ought to be here. He tapped out morse
To the allies during the last World War, and worked out how to vanish

From the Japanese below his polished redwood floor.
Crashing through her roof below, onto Chinese auntie's house,
Out of the air fell a pole. Auction-value decorated tile chairs,
Upon which it must be cool to sit, line up somewhat stiltedly
Next to her favourite rocker. Buddha's swopped his snake for tractor tires

And Michelin Man has become the god of lorries,
Dangling from the mainframe, just behind the front four wheels
Of a triple-decker truck, another's high-backed rear's
Decorated with an attractive spirit of that truck.
Next a truck flies flags at its back: the skull and stripes,

Constellations, crossbones. Skin-brightening solutions
Smile shyly from their ads' gigantic boards.
More of a wall each day around your lake
Sending out rings, now here, now there,
Writhing with tails today – less and less space –

Simply a mess of simmering scales. As the level drops
And turns the lake into a pond, the pond into soup,
Oily-green and thick, a younger generation
Who like to bland each other out, sip gently from *their* soup
In the gated joint above, graced with a water-front

Locale and a fountain of its own. Discussing ice
For the length of the meal without a smile is quite a feat!
You keep chewing in the front of your mouth, just
Behind the lips, ensuring you explore every taste as well
As removing bits you don't intend to eat.

There is this Hindu swing at the portals of Lord Shiva's home
In Bangkok. After Brahma made the world he sent Shiva
To look after it. As the god descended, Nagas bound up the mountains.
Thus the earth was kept intact. After Shiva found the earth
Intact, the Nagas moved to the seas in celebration

And became mermaids. Shiva tries to balance the economy
By keeping living standards down. Cheap labour, lots of gold
Ensures that Lady Bountiful buys into the ritual
Of some monastic sway. Fights between Garuda and the Naga
Wager on aggressive eagle versus snake who slips away.

Edging on eighty, not a jot older in spirit, but more turned on
By the pics than by anything else. You need to come
And can't without uploading them. Randomly clicking away
While memoryless, age has been relatively kind as yet,
Ah, but you're missing the shock, the jolt of your jouissance.

The uprights of the giant swing represent the mountains,
While the circular base of the thing becomes the earth and the seas.
The Brahmins would swing, trying to capture a satchel of cash
Hooked up on one of its posts. Typical high-risk pursuit
Like head-bashing contests, to which they had to put a stop.

Another lost tradition. You were at Lilibet's Coronation.
Still can see the Queen of Tonga, waving through the downpour,
Churchill throwing V signs. Impressed by staring at it more
Later on a screen in a pub off High Street Ken – as it was pink!
And you think, the first time you had ever seen TV. Your eight year life

Already rich in secrets, enchantments, odours and photos.
All-too-strokable textures too, the sweetest tooth, your father's knife,
And if one embraces the wear, tear, and damage
That comes with age, the ubiquity of the know-how
Allows suspected users a degree of afterlife.

The snapper stalks among the leaves then heads for home
With undigested card. You could say the lack of meaning
Served to celebrate the form – as is the case with nonsense.
There is thus a drift to it, too-woo, to everything.
Garlanded Nagas, incense, corrugated iron painted gold,

Vagrants squatting by the kerb, amidst a litter of banana skins
And shreds of mango. Faking homelessness, when they have a perfectly
Good jungle to return to. Sorting through plastic
By the uncleared tables, sharing the backwaters of public spaces
With pigeons, dogs. Monkeys are more pleasing in your photos

Than in real life, and wrecked homes litter the river-bank,
Reduced to concrete sandwiches; the remains of walls,
Floors and ceilings ground together in a spent orgy
Seeping into the water of the ever lower River Kok last February…
Modestly complete your girlfriend's happiness.

Loss of control or at least loss of the illusion of control
Lets what begins as water surge as arrows drinking light.
Absence of self is the hardest, but you would argue
We can find this in the appreciation of weathered items.
Objects as a process. Moving either from or towards nothingness,

The ladies spend their time nattering contentedly in traffic jams,
Happy to be out there with all the other fans of cactuses,
Miniatures, replicas, monuments, statuary, toys,
Convivial personae that freak you out before the pit stop,
Beckoning inflation, or rather inflations, beckoning

To your windscreen, to the sun. Worshippers of air, the Siamese.
Balloon and wind-tunnel enthusiasts, who will pay good baht
For breezy retreats such as the Chardonnay, the Innisfree.
And so the pillars of the swing rise up empty to the sky.
You find this empty frame aniconic, as was once the Buddha.

They should look into it, those smiling candidates
And the one who has no smile whatsoever. Their portraits endlessly
Repeated along straight stretches of mock-European units:
Riviera or Alhambra, or once scrumptious lounge apartments
All stained and tawdry now at their concrete edges.

Already the motorway pillars are developing buttress roots,
Though most of the walk-ways over eight lanes are aptly shaded
With roofs curved over steps at either end or ends
And over the bridge which represents a giant monkey's tail.
You take aim at Siam with your eyes hampered, making the monkey

Bad-tempered. Dangling a bag for titbits from her throat,
Swinging a bag for the to-be-born baby from her meagre waist,
Offering abrupt violence when you get your focus in too close without
An offering of your own. Whereas the hare is hidden, fleet,
The cow docile, the robot waitress warning you

When she's cornering by beeping as she trundles past
The mighty tree writing on the sunset with its ragged knot,
You are as hollow as any tube in a clump of them bambooing
By the road. A lot of stuff you see too suddenly to record.
Then something utterly ugly makes for the perfect shot.

NOTES

THE BALLAD OF THE SANDS, p. 63

This poem is written in a verse-form pioneered by F.T. Prince, where, in a six-line stanza, two rhymes must occur, though in any order, while two lines are at liberty not to rhyme. The form mediates admirably between stricture and freedom.

A WALKER ON THE WALL, p.81

Wentloog Flats is an area between Newport and Cardiff.

Drowning on Dry Land is the title of a hit song by O.V. Wright, a Southern soul man of considerable class.

The palsied earth etc. This is nearly a quote from Richard Lovelace's 'Advice to my Best Brother, Frank'. Scansion and sense demanded certain changes.

MY PART IN THE DOWNFALL OF EVERYTHING, p. 167

Opa – Granddad

'*to grow/Guiltless forever...*' from *Johannes Agricola in Meditation* by Robert Browning.

PNAC – The Project for the New American Century was a neoconservative think tank based in Washington, D.C. that focused on United States foreign policy. It was established 1997.

After Matthew Paris, from a note to the *Flores Historiarum* of Roger of Wendover. Paris was an artist as well as a chronicler. He and William de Brailes are the most celebrated English illuminators of their century. Paris paints a very good elephant, but that this beast was acquired by John – who started a collection of exotic species – is poetic licence. Our first elephant was presented by Louis IX to John's son Henry III and kept in the menagerie at the Tower, along with a leopard and a camel. Returning from the crusades in 1241, Richard Coeur de Lion was welcomed into Cremona by Frederick II's elephant – a gift from the Sultan of Egypt – with trumpeters mounted on its back. Richard treated the kingdom as his milk cow, sold off much of the Royal estate and then had to be ransomed. John however is credited with having invented income tax and was an able administrator – however the church conspired with the barons against him. Since clerics (clerks) were the historians of the time, John has always laboured under a hostile press.

'Astutely regarded his Liege' – made sure that John got a portion of the Emir's gifts.

ACKNOWLEDGEMENTS

'Sergei de Diaghileff' was first printed as a Turret pamphlet in 1968. 'It was then included in *Inside the Castle*, my first collection – from Barrie & Rockliffe in 1969; 'Femina Deserta' was first published as a pamphlet by Softly Loudly Books in 1971. It was subsequently included in *Notions of a Mirror* – my first collection from Anvil (1983). 'Attitudes at Altitudes' and 'Motorway Miniatures' appeared in *Why I may Never See the Walls of China* (Anvil, 1986). 'Boxing the Cleveland' came out in *Howell's Law* – published by Anvil in 1990. 'The Ballad of the Sands' and 'A Walker on the Wall' appeared in *First Time in Japan* – published by Anvil in 1995. 'Border Country' was a commission for the Hay Festival, and was published, together with 'Dancers in Daylight' and 'Beverley at Iguazú' in *Dancers in Daylight* – Anvil, 2003. 'Ode to a Routine' and 'The Ogre's Wife' came out in *The Ogre's Wife* – published by Anvil in 2009. 'Silent Highway' was published in *Silent Highway* by Anvil in 2014. 'My Part in the Downfall of Everything' was first published in *The Fortnightly Review* and later appeared in *From Inside* (High Window Press) together with 'The Delegation'.

SELECTED PUBLICATIONS BY ANTHONY HOWELL

POETRY

Inside the Castle 1969
Imruil 1970
Notions of a Mirror 1983
Why I May Never See the Walls of China 1986
Howell's Law 1990
First Time in Japan 1995
Dancers in Daylight 2003
The Ogre's Wife 2009
Silent Highway 2014
From Inside 2017
Songs of Realisation 2019
Invention of Reality 2022

FICTION

In the Company of Others 1986
Oblivion 2002
Consciousness (with Mutilation) 2002
The Distance Measured in Days 2021

PROSE

The Analysis of Performance Art 1999
Serbian Sturgeon 2000
The Step is the Foot 2019

AS EDITOR

Near Calvary: The Selected Poems of Nicholas Lafitte 1992